An Analysis of

William Wordsworth's

Preface to
The Lyrical Ballads

Alex Latter
with
Rachel Teubner

Published by Macat International Ltd
24:13 Coda Centre, 189 Munster Road, London SW6 6AW.

Distributed exclusively by Routledge
2 Park Square, Milton Park, Abingdon, Oxon OX14 4RN
711 Third Avenue, New York, NY 10017, USA

Routledge is an imprint of the Taylor & Francis Group, an informa business

www.macat.com
info@macat.com

Cataloguing in Publication Data
A catalogue record for this book is available from the British Library.
Library of Congress Cataloguing-in-Publication Data is available upon request.
Cover illustration: Jonathan Edwards

ISBN 978-1-912453-59-7 (hardback)
ISBN 978-1-912453-14-6 (paperback)
ISBN 978-1-912453-29-0 (e-book)

Notice
The information in this book is designed to orientate readers of the work under analysis,
to elucidate and contextualise its key ideas and themes, and to aid in the development
of critical thinking skills. It is not meant to be used, nor should it be used, as a
substitute for original thinking or in place of original writing or research. References and
notes are provided for informational purposes and their presence does not constitute
endorsement of the information or opinions therein. This book is presented solely for
educational purposes. It is sold on the understanding that the publisher is not engaged
to provide any scholarly advice. The publisher has made every effort to ensure that
this book is accurate and up-to-date, but makes no warranties or representations with
regard to the completeness or reliability of the information it contains. The information
and the opinions provided herein are not guaranteed or warranted to produce particular
results and may not be suitable for students of every ability. The publisher shall not be
liable for any loss, damage or disruption arising from any errors or omissions, or from
the use of this book, including, but not limited to, special, incidental, consequential or
other damages caused, or alleged to have been caused, directly or indirectly, by the
information contained within.

Printed and bound by CPI Group (UK) Ltd, Croydon, CR0 4YY

CONTENTS

THE MACAT LIBRARY

The Macat Library is a series of unique academic explorations of seminal works in the humanities and social sciences – books and papers that have had a significant and widely recognised impact on their disciplines. It has been created to serve as much more than just a summary of what lies between the covers of a great book. It illuminates and explores the influences on, ideas of, and impact of that book. Our goal is to offer a learning resource that encourages critical thinking and fosters a better, deeper understanding of important ideas.

Each publication is divided into three Sections: Influences, Ideas, and Impact. Each Section has four Modules. These explore every important facet of the work, and the responses to it.

This Section-Module structure makes a Macat Library book easy to use, but it has another important feature. Because each Macat book is written to the same format, it is possible (and encouraged!) to cross-reference multiple Macat books along the same lines of inquiry or research. This allows the reader to open up interesting interdisciplinary pathways.

To further aid your reading, lists of glossary terms and people mentioned are included at the end of this book (these are indicated by an asterisk [*] throughout) – as well as a list of works cited.

Macat has worked with the University of Cambridge to identify the elements of critical thinking and understand the ways in which six different skills combine to enable effective thinking.
Three allow us to fully understand a problem; three more give us the tools to solve it. Together, these six skills make up the **PACIER** model of critical thinking. They are:

ANALYSIS – understanding how an argument is built
EVALUATION – exploring the strengths and weaknesses of an argument
INTERPRETATION – understanding issues of meaning

CREATIVE THINKING – coming up with new ideas and fresh connections
PROBLEM-SOLVING – producing strong solutions
REASONING – creating strong arguments

To find out more, visit **WWW.MACAT.COM.**

CRITICAL THINKING AND WORDSWORTH'S PREFACE TO *LYRICAL BALLADS*

Primary critical thinking skill: CREATIVE THINKING
Secondary critical thinking skill: PROBLEM SOLVING

Wordsworth's Preface is a good example of how creative expression can captive an audience that might otherwise be unreceptive to a writer's ideas. The central idea of the *Preface to Lyrical Ballads* is that poetry should speak in a language that is natural to humans, and that this language is most abundantly found in the speech and customs of rural life. Poetry, Wordsworth argues, is very different from clever arrangements of words: it is the true language of human emotion, and any human—whether rural or urban, laborer or socialite—can recognize it as the natural language of feeling.

Many of the ideas of the Preface were expressed in a more sophisticated philosophical form by Samuel Taylor Coleridge, the co-author of the original *Lyrical Ballads*. But it was Wordsworth's talent for redefining an issue so as to see it in a new – and more colorfully expressed way – that gave these ideas a special power. Even today, Wordsworth's definition of poetry as the "spontaneous overflow" of human emotion is easy to remember, and hard to refute.

ABOUT THE AUTHOR OF THE ORIGINAL WORK

William Wordsworth (1770-1850) was born in Cockermouth, Cumberland. As a young man, he read contemporary British poetry with admiration, and his travel in France during the Revolution awakened his radical sympathies. These early influences were partly responsible for bringing him into the company of revolutionary thinkers and elite writers and critics in London, where he met Samuel Taylor Coleridge. Wordsworth's friendship with Coleridge became a rich philosophical and literary partnership, resulting in their collaborative, anonymous publication of *Lyrical Ballads* in 1798. Thereafter, Wordsworth wrote prolifically. In 1843, he was appointed Poet Laureate to Queen Victoria.

ABOUT THE AUTHORS OF THE ANALYSIS

Dr. Alex Latter completed his PhD at the Contemporary Poetics Research Centre at Birkbeck, University of London, where his thesis looked at postwar British poetry. He is the author of *Late Modernism and The English Intelligencer: On the Poetics of Community* (2015).

Rachel Teubner is a PhD candidate at the University of Virginia. She teaches courses in Christian thought and in religion and literature, and is the author of *A Macat Analysis of T.S. Eliot's The Sacred Wood* (Routledge, 2014).

ABOUT MACAT

GREAT WORKS FOR CRITICAL THINKING

Macat is focused on making the ideas of the world's great thinkers accessible and comprehensible to everybody, everywhere, in ways that promote the development of enhanced critical thinking skills.

It works with leading academics from the world's top universities to produce new analyses that focus on the ideas and the impact of the most influential works ever written across a wide variety of academic disciplines. Each of the works that sit at the heart of its growing library is an enduring example of great thinking. But by setting them in context – and looking at the influences that shaped their authors, as well as the responses they provoked – Macat encourages readers to look at these classics and game-changers with fresh eyes. Readers learn to think, engage and challenge their ideas, rather than simply accepting them.

'Macat offers an amazing first-of-its-kind tool for interdisciplinary learning and research. Its focus on works that transformed their disciplines and its rigorous approach, drawing on the world's leading experts and educational institutions, opens up a world-class education to anyone.'

Andreas Schleicher
Director for Education and Skills, Organisation for Economic Co-operation and Development

'Macat is taking on some of the major challenges in university education … They have drawn together a strong team of active academics who are producing teaching materials that are novel in the breadth of their approach.'

Prof Lord Broers,
former Vice-Chancellor of the University of Cambridge

'The Macat vision is exceptionally exciting. It focuses upon new modes of learning which analyse and explain seminal texts which have profoundly influenced world thinking and so social and economic development. It promotes the kind of critical thinking which is essential for any society and economy. This is the learning of the future.'

Rt Hon Charles Clarke, former UK Secretary of State for Education

'The Macat analyses provide immediate access to the critical conversation surrounding the books that have shaped their respective discipline, which will make them an invaluable resource to all of those, students and teachers, working in the field.'

Professor William Tronzo, University of California at San Diego

WAYS IN TO THE TEXT

KEY POINTS

* William Wordsworth was an English poet, known for his contributions to the Romantic* movement.
* The Preface announced a new movement in poetry, embracing the value of nature, rural life, and emotion.
* Along with *Lyrical Ballads*, the Preface eventually persuaded writers and critics to welcome the Romantic turn in poetry.

Who was William Wordsworth?

William Wordsworth was born in the Lake District* of England in 1770. His early childhood was financially comfortable, though his well-to-do parents had both died by the time he was thirteen. He was sent to fine English schools and was well trained in literature and European languages, but did not distinguish himself in his studies, and never entered into a formal profession. He travelled in France between 1790 and 1793 as the French Revolution* was unfolding, and the egalitarian principles of French radicals awakened his sympathy. When war broke out between England and France, Wordsworth was forced to return to England, leaving behind his lover, Annette Vallon, and daughter Anne-Caroline, and as the Revolution became increasingly destructive, Wordsworth's radical sympathies began to wane. Returning to the Lake District, he lived with his sister Dorothy Wordsworth* and struck up a rich and productive friendship with the poet and critic Samuel Taylor Coleridge.* From 1797 to 1807—often called his "great decade"— Wordsworth wrote the poems that quickly made him famous in Britain, and for which he is still best known. In the Preface to his collection *Lyrical Ballads*, he announced a new movement in poetry, and these works are indeed widely regarded as the beginning of the Romantic movement in British poetry.

In 1802 he married Mary Hutchinson, with whom he had four children. He became a noted defender of the pristine beauty of the Lake District, actively opposing the intrusion of railways. Wordsworth enjoyed wide celebrity in the last decade of his life, eventually becoming Poet Laureate* to Queen Victoria.* He died in 1850.

What does the Preface say?

Wordsworth's Preface argues that poetry is the natural human language. Unlike the highly rhetorical mock-heroic poetry that was pervasively acclaimed in eighteenth-century Britain, Wordsworth claimed, poetry should attend primarily to the essential human passions and to humanity's relationship to the natural world. These poetic materials are abundant in rural life; hence rural life, rather than the sophisticated lives of prominent city-dwellers, offers a style and a subject extraordinarily appropriate to poetry.

The Preface was intended to offer a defence of *Lyrical Ballads,* a collection of poetry that Wordsworth and Samuel Taylor Coleridge had first published anonymously in 1798. This collection intentionally celebrated rural life and experimented with traditional forms of popular poetry, such as the ballad. This first edition of *Lyrical Ballads* sold out quickly, and Wordsworth soon began working on a second edition. The new 1800 edition, however, was markedly different from the first, both in presentation and content. It was published under

Wordsworth's name in two volumes, and the new additions and revisions resulted in a collection that primarily featured Wordsworth's poems and only a few of Coleridge's. Moreover, the new edition included a lengthy Preface, written by Wordsworth, that explained the theory behind the experimental approach and rustic style of these poems. However, the Preface was intended to do more than offer interpretive aids to readers of the *Ballads*; it also announced a new poetics*—an aesthetic and ethical vision for poetry—that was intended to revolutionize British poetry.

As the second edition began to circulate and the critics began to respond, Wordsworth began further revisions, including a long insertion into the Preface, for yet another edition of *Lyrical Ballads*. The Preface and the *Ballads* went on to enjoy still further editions and republications, but this third edition, which appeared in 1802, is generally regarded as the fullest expression of Wordsworth's intentions for the Preface. For that reason, it is the 1802 Preface that is usually discussed in contemporary scholarship, and it is the 1802 Preface that is the focus of this book.

The basis for the style and lexicon of the *Ballads* is the language of the rural laborer, rather than the language of social elites. Wordsworth's vision for poetry extends far beyond these poems; in the Preface, he announces a new poetic language that bears closer relation to language as it is actually spoken, and that will revolutionize British poetry forever. This new poetry, he argues, will heighten the sense of kinship between different layers of society. In the new age of poetry, poets will be far more than wordsmiths: their role is to renew human sympathy by speaking in a language that reveals the conditions common to all humans. Poetry, likewise, is not the elite language of the classically educated, but the language of emotion: its source is "the spontaneous overflow of powerful feelings... recollected in tranquility."[1] Though not everyone agreed, the claims of the Preface eventually came to be regarded as a transitional

11

moment in English poetry. The new movement that the Preface announced came to be known as Romanticism, and poets and critics have turned to the Preface ever since to define their own poetic ideals.

Why does the Preface matter?

Wordsworth's account of the "true nature" of poetic language and the poetic vocation has had an enormous influence on the composition and the study of English poetry. The Preface made claims for a kind of poetry and a way of living that had previously been regarded as too vulgar, too unrefined, for real literary treatment. While the ballad and other popular forms of poetry had attracted some attention in the late eighteenth century, the Preface conferred an altogether new status on these genres, on their language and on the lives that they celebrated. Wordsworth's claim that poetry was the language of real human emotion, moreover, was taken up by a new generation of Romantic poets who shared his vision for a poetry of experience and emotion.

The Preface to *Lyrical Ballads* has remained central to the definition of British Romanticism. No one document could be said to comprehend the entire movement; but the Preface expresses many of the key concepts—the revelatory power of nature, the imaginative richness of experience, the human essence linking all humans to one another—that characterizes a great deal of the work that we now describe as Romantic. Its influence can be seen both in the work of the poets of subsequent generations, and in the understanding of the Romantic movement that has provoked academic debate ever since.

Wordsworth's work in the Preface also represents the beginning of a significant cultural moment. In the nineteenth century, writers and readers across northern Europe and America were beginning to be attracted to the individual authority of experience and imagination, and to nature as a place of revelation and as a remedy to living and working conditions in cities that were rapidly becoming industrialized.

Contemporary ideas about nature as a place of revelation and of restoration, and about the power of human experience, are in various ways anticipated in Wordsworth's Preface. In this sense, both the Preface and the *Lyrical Ballads* represent a point of transition from the Enlightenment* to the Romantic era, and starting point for many of our modern concerns. The endurance of Wordsworth's definition of poetry as "feelings…recollected in tranquility" is a piece of evidence that his insights in the Preface have yet to be superseded. Wordsworth is one of the earliest poets in English to anticipate the voice and the concerns of modernity.

NOTES

1   William Wordsworth, "Preface" *Lyrical Ballads: 1798 and 1802*, ed. Fiona Stafford (Oxford: Oxford University Press, 2013), 111.

SECTION 1
INFLUENCES

MODULE 1
THE AUTHOR AND THE
HISTORICAL CONTEXT

KEY POINTS

- The Preface is now regarded as the definitive manifesto of Romantic poetry.
- William Wordsworth was an educated Englishman from the Lake District.
- Industrialization, the French Revolution, and the rapid urbanization of British cities all powerfully shaped Wordsworth's historical context.

Why Read This Text?

The Preface to *Lyrical Ballads* is a statement of Wordsworth's poetic vision, one that would come to define the poetics of Romantic writers. First published as an accompaniment to the second edition of *Lyrical Ballads* (1800), the Preface offered an explanation of the poetic process behind the poems. But in addition to serving as a commentary on the poems, the Preface announced a new movement in poetry, based on a new definition of poetic language and of the poetic calling.

The popularity of *Lyrical Ballads*, and the critical acclaim that Wordsworth's poetry eventually won, mark the importance of the Preface as a commentary on the subjects and aesthetics of Wordsworth's work at the height of his literary powers. As a product of the intellectual and literary collaboration between Wordsworth and the writer Samuel Taylor Coleridge, the Preface is a centerpiece of the radical new literary vision generated by their notorious friendship.

To the generation of Romantic writers that emerged in its wake, however, the Preface offered far more than mere insights into the

66 The seriousness of the new Preface was not merely a result of irritation over reviews of the first edition. The return to England in 1799 had coincided with one of the darkest phases of international experience, as the thrilling revolutionary energies of the French turned into expansive, imperialist ambitions, while at home, food shortages, high prices, and endless demand for new recruits drove ordinary farmers to despair... 99

Fiona Stafford, "Introduction" to *Lyrical Ballads, 1798 and 1802*

Lyrical Ballads and its authors. Wordsworth's Preface eventually was hailed as the harbinger of a literary movement that had changed English poetry altogether. It announced a new understanding of the creative process and of the high purposes of poetry: to reveal the human condition, and to awaken in its readers the profoundest emotions and the most enduring truths of existence. Its aesthetic vision exalted the everyday themes of rural life and the role of the natural world in revealing those truths. The *Lyrical Ballads* themselves offered a persuasive realization of Wordsworth's manifesto, and the Preface's declarations have come to represent an aesthetic vision that forever changed the way that poetry in English was written and understood.

Author's Life

Wordsworth was born in 1770, in Cockermouth, Cumbria. His early life was marked by extraordinary privilege, radical tastes, and tragic upheavals. Wordsworth was the son of wealthy parents, both of whom had died by the time he was thirteen years old. He was educated at excellent schools, Hawkshead, and St John's College, Cambridge, but failed both to distinguish himself at school and to enter a recognizable profession. Despite his mediocre performance at school, Wordsworth was an impressive student of Latin and Italian and knew much of English poetry by heart, and as a young man he made his way easily among the literary elites of his day. His political tendencies in his early life were revolutionary and populist, and his philosophical instincts led him away from the established Church and toward Unitarianism and atheism.[1]

Wordsworth travelled extensively through France in the years after the Revolution, but became disillusioned by the violence that followed in its wake and the subsequent war between Britain and France. He returned to England in 1793, leaving behind him his partner Annette Vallon and his daughter Anne-Caroline. In England, he was reunited with his sister, Dorothy Wordsworth, from whom he had been mostly separated since early childhood, and the two Wordsworths set up house together in Keswick in 1794. The Wordsworths remained primarily resident in the Lake District of England throughout their lives, and the images and themes of William Wordsworth's poetry were powerfully shaped by rural life and by the pristine beauty of the region. In this context Wordsworth formed a close friendship with Samuel Taylor Coleridge, inaugurating the collaboration that would generate the vision and the poems that became *Lyrical Ballads*.

Author's Background

The *Ballads* marked the beginning of the most productive decade of Wordsworth's literary life, and the period of what most consider his greatest work. Following his marriage to Mary Hutchinson in 1802, Wordsworth was increasingly occupied with family life and with revisions of his earlier work, and his political and religious affiliations gradually lost their radical edge. He became a civil servant, actively supported Tory politics and the Church of England, and was eventually named Poet Laureate to Queen Victoria. Yet his changing loyalties did not disguise the poetic and humanitarian impulses that remained consistent throughout his life: the revelatory power of the imaginative life and the value of the natural world in its unspoiled form.

In its valorization of rustic life and language, the Preface is in many ways a response to the political context of the 1790s. Britain was at war with France, food was scarce, and urban poverty was increasingly conspicuous. A decade before, the radical promises of the French Revolution had inspired Wordsworth, Coleridge, and a generation of young elites to cultivate passionate sympathies and hopes. But these promises had soured in the wake of the Revolution and the rise of the French republic's imperial ambitions. In the meantime, British cities were rapidly industrializing, and the whole country had begun to experience a population drift from the countryside to the city centers. The forms of life and language that Wordsworth discusses in the Preface represent an alternate point from which a more equable, human social organization might emerge. Wordsworth saw the poems collected in *Lyrical Ballads* as endowed with the high purpose of revealing the human essence to be found in nature, and building a common bond of sympathy between all people. In this sense, the Preface can be read as a literary outworking of the populist instincts that had earlier been energized, and then disappointed, by the Revolution.

NOTES

1   Nicola Trott, "Wordsworth: the shape of the poetic career," in *The Cambridge Companion to Wordsworth* (Cambridge: Cambridge University Press, 2003), 5-6.

MODULE 2
ACADEMIC CONTEXT

KEY POINTS

- In the late eighteenth century, literary critics largely favored an artificial style, influenced by classical models.
- The political revolutions of the late eighteenth century, particularly the revolution in France, captured the imagination of young British intellectuals.
- The rustic poets that Wordsworth read at a young age, and the political thought of William Godwin,* were formative academic influences.

The Work in its Context

The literary tastes of the eighteenth century generally favored a highly formalized style of poetry. Both literary critics and school curricula of this period reflect a preference for classical poets such as Virgil and Horace. The success of the poet Alexander Pope,* who won acclaim and a wide readership with *The Rape of the Lock,* marked the appearance of the mock-heroic style, which both imitated and cleverly poked fun at the rhetorical devices and lofty themes of classical epics. As Wordsworth was coming of age, imitators of Pope's parodic style were capitalizing on the tastes of the moment, which were in turn being passed down in schools and magazines. At the same time, however, traditional, popular verse forms had begun to find a literary readership. One such example was the ballad, a traditional English verse form that told a story, often a simple tale of rural life involving love or untimely death. The popularity of the ballad exemplified a more general enthusiasm for "rustic" poetry, and in this context a number of "peasant poets" had risen to momentary fame.[1] Prior to the appearance in 1798

> ❝ In retrospect, it is possible to see how significant it is that Wordsworth was early reading Cowper, Smith and Burns. By the 1780s, with the big figures Gray, Collins and Goldsmith gone, it must have seemed to some that poetry had lost its way: Pope's imitators thronged the periodicals and newspapers, but even the best of them lacked his originality. Ornamented and artificial in style, they imitated the classical models, mused on abstraction, and meditated on spiritual matters. For the moment, poetry was closeted in the drawing room, where it bore little on the outside world. ❞
>
> Duncan Wu, "Wordsworth's poetry to 1798"

of the *Lyrical Ballads,* however, no poet had attempted to write in the rustic style of these popular forms with the aspiration of finding critical acclaim in literary culture.

Overview of the Field

In the latter half of the eighteenth century, the Western world at large had experienced a broad pattern of dramatic political revolution, most famously in America and in France. Both revolutions, despite their very different results, demonstrated a sudden turn from monarchial rule to democratic representation, and in their different ways, they caught the world's imagination. Wordsworth and Coleridge were just two members of a new generation, including but not limited to social elites, that saw the appeal of a new social order and an erasure of powerful hierarchies that previously seemed unthinkable.

The publication of William Godwin's *Political Justice* in 1795 marks a defining moment for the political radicalism of Wordsworth's generation, as well as for Wordsworth himself. Godwin's political idealism presented a rational alternative to the violent upheavals of the post-revolutionary Terror in France, arguing that social progress could be achieved through reason alone. While the sway of his enlightened ideals did not last long, Godwin did exercise a powerful influence on London political activity in the last years of the eighteenth century, both through his work and as a London personality who kept company with reformers and radicals. Energizing a revolutionary spirit, Godwin's doctrines of social improvement and of the freedom of the individual mind appealed powerfully to those caught up in the new spirit of democracy. But in the years that followed, many of Godwin's enthusiasts found their zeal waning, and, like Wordsworth, began searching for yet another democratic vision.

Academic Influences

From an early age, Wordsworth's literary imagination was fueled by his exposure at Hawkshead Grammar School to contemporary poets such as William Cowper,* Charlotte Smith,* and Robert Burns.* This exposure, while consistent with the preferences of later generations, was unusual at the time. Literary taste and school curricula favored classical poetry and classical imitators almost exclusively; Virgil and Horace were taught alongside Alexander Pope and his imitators.[2] Wordsworth's education departed from this contemporary preference for abstraction and stylistic artifice, apprenticing him instead to poets of experience who took up the themes of everyday life. While not strictly representative of his immediate cultural context, this formation can certainly be understood as an early reaction against it, presaging the literary revolutions Wordsworth would eventually inspire.

During his time in France, Wordsworth had been caught up in the revolutionary fervor that surrounded him, and for a time his sympathies were staunchly aligned with the French radical cause. However, in the early 1790s, as the revolution became increasingly menacing, Wordsworth's enthusiasm was fading. William Godwin's philosophic rationalism presented what seemed a peaceable alternative to violent political revolution. After reading Godwin's *Political Justice* in the mid 1790s, Wordsworth became a fervent Godwinian, seeking out Godwin and other radicals in London and taking part, for a time, in their intellectual habits and community.[3] This revolutionary vision was also, ultimately, a disappointment to Wordsworth.[4] Neither political force, nor philosophical argument, seemed sufficient to the revolutionary change that Wordsworth felt was needed in British society. In the late 1790s he found himself in search of a new humanitarian ideal, a new code to live by.

NOTES

1   Scott McEathron, "Wordsworth, Lyrical Ballads, and the Problem of Peasant Poetry," *Nineteenth-Century Literature* 54.1 (1999), 1-4.

2   Duncan Wu, "Wordsworth's poetry to 1798," in *The Cambridge Companion to Wordsworth*, ed. Stephen Gill, (Cambridge: Cambridge University Press, 2003), 22-23.

3   Nicholas Roe, "Politics, history, and Wordsworth's poems," in *The Cambridge Companion to Wordsworth,* ed. Stephen Gill, (Cambridge: Cambridge University Press, 2003), 198-199.

4   Seamus Perry, "Wordsworth and Coleridge," in *The Cambridge Companion to Wordsworth,* ed. Stephen Gill, (Cambridge: Cambridge University Press, 2003), 162.

MODULE 3
THE PROBLEM

KEY POINTS

- The French revolution prompted Wordsworth's generation to reconsider notions of equality and of human progress.

- A turn toward traditional and popular forms manifested a similar interest in democracy.

- The Preface first appeared as clarification of the aesthetic ideals of the original collection that Wordsworth and Coleridge had published.

Core Question

In the late eighteenth century, northern Europe experienced two major political revolutions. The first was the victory of the American colonies that claimed independence from British rule, building a new nation as the United States of America. The second revolution played out on European soil, when the French people, motivated by untenable working and living conditions as well as by egalitarian ideals, began to organize in support of political reforms. As the eighteenth century came to a close, the new American nation was engaged with its own difficulties of setting up a democratic republic, founded on the ideal of the equal status of all people; meanwhile, the early triumphs of the revolutionary project in France were followed within a few years by the trial and execution of the king and queen, massacre, violence, and widespread fear, as leaders tried and failed to introduce new political orders and to consolidate power. By the time Wordsworth returned to England, the French had become an imperialist threat to its neighboring countries. These historical events are now so well known that they can easily be taken for granted as unshakeable realities.

> **❝** ...for if Wordsworth's career and ambition as a poet are simply unthinkable without Coleridge, then Coleridge's thinking about literature and the imagination is similarly inconceivable without the provocative example of Wordsworth's genius. At their first acquaintance, however, in Bristol in September 1795, they met not as poet and critic, nor even as two poets exactly, but rather as two friends of liberty, caught up in the continuing ideological excitement that followed the revolution in France. **❞**
>
> Seamus Perry, "Wordsworth and Coleridge"

However, to contemporary Britain, political revolution had come as a shock, and was seen to pose an immediate threat to national and economic security. For those who experienced them firsthand as Wordsworth did, the terrifying realities of the French revolution were enough to make even the most idealistic young egalitarians wary of toppling the existing orders.

The questions at the heart of the political and philosophical debates of the 1790s, then, interrogated notions of human flourishing and social progress: how should society be organized? How could humans be free and equal, and yet also protected from the abuses of power that seemed almost inevitable? What were the resources—religious, scientific, or institutional—best suited to advance human progress?

The Participants

Wordsworth's historical and political context must be understood as powerfully shaped by the experience of political revolution. For Wordsworth and many other members of the literary elite, such experiences led directly to literary debates concerning the nature of poetry, the operations of the creative process, and the relationship of poetry to revelation and experience. While these questions might appear to be relevant only to poetry, they actually are part of a much broader cultural pattern of reflection on the value of conventions—be they social or literary—and of the institutions that alleged to maintain social order. In the late eighteenth century, France, the United States, and the Europeans who looked on admiringly were caught up in the spirit of democracy, of granting to all humans the status and representation that was their due. In the world of literary publishing and reading, however, a literary turn toward traditional popular forms manifested the same instinct: to recognize the value not merely of well-born, well-educated, or wealthy members of society, but of the everyman and the everyman's voice. New printed collections of ballads by Thomas Percy* and other "rustic" writers found a literary audience for the stories and the language of everyday life.[1] But unlike Wordsworth, such writers tended to celebrate folk traditions without innovation. The turn toward popular forms was, in many ways, a call for the voice of the people. Yet until the publication of *Lyrical Ballads,* nothing resembling a revolution of poetic form had taken place; the poems being introduced to British readers represented a tradition that had not yet been subject to Wordsworth's experiments.

The Contemporary Debate

Wordsworth first met Samuel Taylor Coleridge through the radical social and intellectual circles of London, in which Coleridge was a prominent figure.[2] Both writers had initially been swept up in the egalitarian ideals of the French Revolution, and then badly disappointed. Around the time that they met, Wordsworth's Godwinian phase was coming to an end, and Coleridge became his new philosophical mentor and literary collaborator. *Lyrical Ballads* was the fruit of this friendship, and the philosophical ideals underpinning the collection were in many ways an answer to the questions of equality and human flourishing that had been raised by the Revolution.

The original version of *Lyrical Ballads* that appeared in 1798 represented a more or less equal partnership between Wordsworth and Samuel Taylor Coleridge, who divided the labor of the original collection between them. But the egalitarian vision of their experimental poems was not everywhere understood by its readers, and *Lyrical Ballads* initially met with a mixed reception. Perhaps the most significant review it received was from Robert Southey,* who wrote that "the experiment has failed, not because the language of conversation is little adapted to 'the purposes of poetic pleasure,' but because it has been tried upon uninteresting subjects."[3] Southey's criticism is representative of the prevailing literary tastes of the day for a more highly stylized poetry, depicting people of high social standing in the grand style of classical epic poetry. Southey's criticism also seems to have offered at least partial motivation for the Preface, which first appeared as an introduction to the second edition that appeared in 1800. The Preface offered a justification of its subjects, one much more thorough than the brief Advertisement that had accompanied the first edition. The Preface thus represents Wordsworth's reinforced and expanded declaration of the original vision, shared by Wordsworth and Coleridge, of *Lyrical Ballads*: to reveal the literary power of the common voice and the natural beauty of everyday life.

NOTES

1   Fiona Stafford, "Introduction" *Lyrical Ballads: 1798 and 1802,* William Wordsworth and Samuel Coleridge, ed. Fiona Stafford (Oxford: Oxford University Press, 2013), ··.

2   Seamus Perry, "Wordsworth and Coleridge," in *The Cambridge Companion to Wordsworth,* ed. Stephen Gill (Cambridge: Cambridge University Press, 2003), 162.

3   Robert Southey, *The Romantics Reviewed: Part A, The Lake Poets*, Vol. 1. (New York: Harman, 1972), 310.

MODULE 4
THE AUTHOR'S CONTRIBUTION

KEY POINTS

- In writing the Preface, Wordsworth intended to explain the volume's choice of subject, but also to announce a new, revolutionary kind of poetry.

- The Preface approached the matter of human equality and sympathy as a poetic question.

- The ideas of the Preface were powerfully shaped by Samuel Taylor Coleridge and by the literary community that formed around Coleridge and Wordsworth.

Author's Aims

Wordsworth's explicit intention in the Preface to *Lyrical Ballads* was to defend the volume's experimental approach to poetry by establishing the principles that underpinned its composition. But this provocation also became a platform for Wordsworth to announce a much wider ambition: to effect a change in the prevailing standards of literary taste in England at the turn of the nineteenth century by setting out new defining criteria for poetic diction and for the character of the poet. His aims were not exclusively literary, however: through a revaluation of the standards of literary taste, the Preface expresses an aspiration for poetry to produce a pleasure in its readers that in turns heighten its readers' sympathy for humanity. Wordworth's ideal poet spreads "relationship and love" and "binds together by passion and knowledge the vast empire of human society."[1] Though his support for dramatic political revolution had waned, Wordsworth's hope for new social and cultural relations was undaunted.

> 66 The principal object, then, which I proposed to myself in these Poems was to chuse incidents and situations from common life, and to relate or describe them, throughout, as far as was possible, in a selection of language really used by men; and, at the same time, to throw over them a certain colouring of the imagination, whereby ordinary things should be presented to the mind in an unusual way; and, further, and above all, to make these incidents and situations interesting by tracing in them, truly though not ostentatiously, the primary laws of our nature… 99
>
> Wordsworth, "Preface"

In the Preface, Wordsworth situates *Lyrical Ballads* as marking a decisive break with the poetic tastes of the eighteenth century. Readers, he warns, will note a sharp contrast between *Lyrical Ballads* and "the gaudiness and inane phraseology of modern writers."[2] For Wordsworth, Thomas Gray's* "Sonnet on the Death of Richard West" exemplifies the artificiality that characterized the dominant style of English poetry in the eighteenth century. In reality, Gray was only one of a number of poets—most of them now rarely read—who aspired to imitate the successes of Alexander Pope's mock-heroic style, itself an imitation of the epic poetry of ancient Greek and Latin poets. Wordsworth's Preface explicitly rejected the social decadence and the stylistic flourishes of the mock-heroic writers and the economic and social elitism of the world that such work tended to project.

Approach

The Preface to *Lyrical Ballads* offers an answer, broadly speaking, to the question of how humankind might progress toward greater sympathy, harmony, and freedom. Its concerns must be understood as responding to the upheaval of social and economic conventions in France, and to the infectious French revolutionary commitment to *libertè, fraternitè,* and *egalitè* (freedom, brotherhood, and equality). By the time he wrote the Preface, however, Wordsworth's political commitments had been largely redirected toward poetry. The question of human equality is in many ways at the heart of *Lyrical Ballads* and of the Preface that defended it. But Wordsworth redefined this question by considering it in literary terms. Instead of asking how political institutions might be democratically organized, the Preface asks: what sort of poetry affirms human equality? What does the voice of the people sound like? And what is the role of the poet with respect to humankind? In short, the Preface takes a political question and offers a poetic solution.

Wordsworth moves through several stages in his argument: first, he describes the object of poetry as close attention to and sympathy with the natural world and humanity's relationship to it, before proposing a poetic language that bears closer relation to language as it is actually spoken. Such a realignment of poetic language will, he argues, have the effect of heightening the sense of kinship between different layers of society. This leads Wordsworth to the question: "What is a Poet?" His answer, in short, is that a poet is "a man speaking to men."[3] In other words, poetry speaks in the natural language of experience that is common to all humans; it is "the spontaneous overflow of powerful feelings ... recollected in tranquility."[4] In expressing the natural feeling that all humans share, poetry offers the true basis for human sympathy. In the figure of the poet, and in this new, common language of poetry, Wordsworth hoped to recover a sense of the optimism he had felt at the dawn of the Revolution.

Contribution in Context

Although it is attributed to Wordsworth's sole authorship, Coleridge's ideas are deeply impressed on the Preface. Coleridge later claimed that it was "half a child of my own brain";[5] Wordsworth stated years later that he wrote it entirely at Coleridge's suggestion. Given his contributions to the original conception and labors of the *Lyrical Ballads* and the intensity of his friendship with Wordsworth during these years, Coleridge's influence on the Preface that defended the collection is certainly pervasive, and cannot be easily divided from Wordsworth's labors.

Besides representing a richly generative partnership with Coleridge, the Preface is also the result of the literary community of which Coleridge and the Wordsworths were an integral part. Dorothy Wordsworth, who copied out the Preface in October 1800, offered critical assistance, but it would be wrong to cast her simply as her brother's scribe: as her journals show, her own receptivity to language and the world around her was finely attuned and often fascinatingly resonant with her brother's work.[6] Wordsworth was at this time frequently visited by writers and critics such as William Hazlitt*— whose conversation inspired Wordsworth to write "Expostulation and Reply" and "The Tables Turned," the poems that opened the revised edition of 1800—and the essayist Thomas de Quincey.* Brought together by unconventional literary tastes and radical political affiliations, these writers constituted a kind of workshop for the new poetics animating the *Lyrical Ballads* and the Preface.

NOTES

1   William Wordsworth, "Preface" *Lyrical Ballads: 1798 and 1802*, ed. Fiona Stafford (Oxford: Oxford University Press, 2013), 106-107.

2   Wordsworth, "Preface" *Lyrical Ballads: 1798 and 1802*, 96.

3   Wordsworth, "Preface" *Lyrical Ballads: 1798 and 1802,* 103.

4   Wordsworth, "Preface" *Lyrical Ballads: 1798 and 1802,* 111.

5   Coleridge to Robert Southey, July 29, 1802, in *Collected Letters: Vol. II, 1801-1806,* ed. Earl Leslie Griggs, (Oxford: Oxford University Press, 2002 [1802]), 830.

6   See, for example, Dorothy Wordsworth, *The Grasmere and Alfoxden Journals*, ed. Pamela Woof, (Oxford: Oxford University Press, 2002), 142.

SECTION 2
IDEAS

MODULE 5
MAIN IDEAS

KEY POINTS

- The Preface explains that rural life forms the subject and the language of *Lyrical Ballads*.
- In the Preface Wordsworth offers a new definition of poetry: it is the "spontaneous overflow" of emotion.
- The Preface claims that *Lyrical Ballads* embodies a new movement in poetry, which will awaken human sympathy in its readers.

Key Themes

The Preface to *Lyrical Ballads* is organized around four basic questions. The first two questions that Wordsworth addresses have to do with the poems collected in the volume: First, why do these poems take rural life as their subject? Second, how should readers understand the style of these poems?

In response to the first question, Wordsworth explains why *Lyrical Ballads* takes up scenes from the life of the rural laborer, rather than from the lives of the urbane leisure classes. Rural life, Wordsworth argues, offers "better soil" for human passions: in this humbler context, the emotions and affections that all humans have in common are cultivated and called on far more than in the social lives and occupations of sophisticated city-dwellers. This theme of the value of the rural life leads Wordsworth directly to his second question: the style of these poems rejects the abstractions and elaborate rhetorical flourishes of highly formalized poetry, in favor of the everyday speech of the rural laborer. This everyday speech, Wordsworth claims, represents the most natural and the best part of language.

> ❝ ...in spite of difference of soil and climate, of language and manners, of laws and customs, in spite of things silently gone out of mind and things violently destroyed, the Poet binds together by passion and knowledge the vast empire of human society, as it is spread over the whole earth, and over all time. ❞
>
> Wordsworth, "Preface"

Following this discussion, Wordsworth takes up two grander questions about poetry itself: What is a poet? And, finally, what is poetry? A poet, Wordsworth claims, speaks as one human to another, defending and upholding human nature, "carrying everywhere relationship and love."[1] To be a poet, then, is a profoundly humane occupation: poets bear a responsibility to reveal the human condition and the connections among all living things. In making these revelations, the work of the poet furthermore awakens in its readers a natural sympathy and compassion for their fellow humans.

In the final section of the Preface, Wordsworth offers his definition of poetry, with a sentence that remains one of his most quoted and most influential claims : "Poetry is the spontaneous overflow of powerful feelings: it takes its origin from emotion recollected in tranquility."[2] The passionate nature of poetic feeling, which is organized and structured by the mechanical operations of poetic meter, perfectly matches the excessive nature of human feeling which is tempered and sifted in the process of recollection.

Exploring the Ideas

The central idea of Wordsworth's Preface is that poetry is a natural language. True poetry speaks in the language of human experience, opening its readers to the profoundest elements of their nature. Poetry should not be governed by rhetorical rules; it is not decorative; it should not be ornate. Instead, poetry must be understood, read and heard as a language as ordinary as a breath, drawing deeply on the feelings and experiences that are vital to being human and shared by all humans.

For Wordsworth, the context of rural life offers a powerful, fresh alternative to the scenes typical of British poetry at the time. The leading poetry of the eighteenth century often drew on scenes from a drawing-room, involving royal or aristocratic figures in situations of political glory and abundant wealth. The style of this leading poetry was as excessive as its subject, highly ornamental and heavy with allusions to Greek and Roman deities and heroes. The prevailing poetry of the day, in Wordsworth's view, was as distant from ordinary human experience as it was unlike ordinary human speech. In both experience and language, it was artificial and unnatural. Scenes from rural life, by contrast, offered the very essence of what it meant to be human, to be connected to other humans and to other living things, to find enduring beauty in lakes and wildflowers and mountains. Similarly, for Wordsworth the language of rural life is itself the natural language of human experience: the way that the rural laborer speaks, and the common objects—stones, fences, trees—that his speech describes convey the emotions and depths of feeling and experience in which *all* humans share.

In this sense, the Preface presents *Lyrical Ballads* as poems exemplifying its poetic ideals. The poems in *Lyrical Ballads,* Wordsworth says, speak in the language of everyday life, a language found in the speech and habits of the rural laborer. These poems, furthermore, point to a new future for poetry, in which poets understanding their calling as a deeply humane task. The effect of *Lyrical Ballads* should be to awaken humans to their shared condition and to establish loving relationships among them; and this awakening is itself the central task of the poet.

Language and Expression

The Preface seeks to effect a change in the prevailing tastes of British poetry. Wordsworth makes an example of those tastes as reflected in Thomas Gray's "Sonnet on the Death of Mr Richard West." Gray* was a poet with a sizeable contemporary audience whose work demonstrated the poetic tendencies Wordsworth saw as most problematic: its language was highly ornate, and its subjects were trivial. The prevailing popularity of poets like Gray also explains something of the defensive tone that occasionally appears in the Preface: Wordsworth often responds to anticipated criticisms, which seem to draw on the perspectives of Wordsworth's imagined readers.

For a twenty-first century reader, it may initially seem odd that a text celebrating "the real language of men" uses a language as elevated and formal as the Preface. It is important to remember, however, that Wordsworth was determined to persuade a literary readership of the value of his new poetic vision. The Preface was in many ways as important for this ambition as the *Lyrical Ballads* themselves, and Wordsworth's primary hope in writing the Preface was to make a formal argument that would convince any reader who had not already been captivated by the poems themselves. Given this formality, it is particularly remarkable that two of Wordsworth's phrases in the Preface remain in constant use: his description of poetry as "the spontaneous overflow of powerful feelings," and of poetry's origin as "emotion recollected in tranquility." These descriptions have been subject to criticism; but the fact that writers and critics continually appeal to them is indicative of their endurance.

NOTES

1   William Wordsworth, "Preface" *Lyrical Ballads: 1798 and 1802*, ed. Fiona Stafford (Oxford: Oxford University Press, 2013), 106.

2   Wordsworth, "Preface" *Lyrical Ballads: 1798 and 1802,* 111.

MODULE 6
SECONDARY IDEAS

KEY POINTS

* The Preface criticizes the living and working conditions of a rapidly industrializing Britain.
* The Preface proposes that poetry is the antidote to the problems caused by industrialization.
* Wordsworth's understanding of the complementary relationship between science and poetry has largely been overlooked.

Other Ideas

Behind the Preface's primary concern with poetry itself lies a quiet criticism of the social and economic conditions of modern life in Britain. The Industrial Revolution had exercised seemingly inexorable changes, drawing people out of rural villages and the countryside and into increasingly crowded cities. Such changes wrought havoc not only on the living and working conditions of laborers, but on the imagination and the "discriminating powers of the mind."[1] Wordsworth himself had experienced great personal renewal in moving to the Lake District, and the appearance of *Lyrical Ballads*, which had its genesis in Wordsworth's long walks around the Quantocks with Coleridge, offered to Wordsworth a piece of positive evidence: these poems indicated the salutary effects of country life on his own creative imagination. Thus, while the Preface primarily emphasizes the value of rural life as good soil for human emotion, and thus good soil for poetry, it also makes the case that life outside of cities is better suited to a generally flourishing humanity.

> ❝ For a multitude of causes, unknown to former times, are now acting with a combined force to blunt the discriminating powers of the mind, and unfitting it for all voluntary exertion to reduce it to a state of almost savage torpor. The most effective of these causes are the great national events which are daily taking place, and the increasing accumulation of men in cities, where the uniformity of their occupations produces a craving for extraordinary incident, which the rapid communication of intelligence hourly gratifies. To this tendency of life and manners the literature and theatrical exhibitions of the country have conformed themselves... ❞
> Wordsworth, "Preface"

The Preface also offers an extended reflection on the relationship between poets and scientists. The endeavors of poetry and science have important things in common: both aspire to knowledge as forms of human pleasure. This similarity also reveals an important difference: knowledge via poetry reveals human nature, but knowledge via science is discrete and cannot tell us anything about humanity itself. According to Wordsworth, science finds expression in poetry, because it is "the breath and finer spirit of all knowledge; it is the impassioned expression which is in the countenance of all Science."[2] Rather than figuring science and poetry as irreconcilable opposites, he imagines a time when the "remotest discoveries of the Chemist, the Botanist, or Mineralogist, will be as proper objects of the Poet's art as any upon which it can be employed."[3] Far from opposing the discoveries of modern science to the riches of the poetic imagination, Wordsworth envisages a complementary relationship between them.

Exploring the Ideas

Wordsworth's vision of rural life as the antidote to the ills of industrialization is intimately related to his vision for poetry. Wordsworth's aspirations for *Lyrical Ballads* are primarily literary, and in the Preface he is at pains to emphasize that he sees the *Ballads* as inaugurating a new movement in poetry specifically. But this literary aspiration also has political implications. In proclaiming that poetry was a natural language, establishing common bonds among fellow humans, Wordsworth was also declaring that all humans were endowed with equal dignity. This point, Wordsworth's hope for political revolution by popular revolt had faded, but he remained committed to the French revolutionaries' democratic principles of *liberté, fraternité,* and *égalité* (freedom, brotherhood, and equality). The Preface expresses this commitment to human equality, and occasionally the Preface offers specifically social criticisms of the effects of mass urbanization on the minds of the general population. In this new vision Wordsworth conceives democracy and human fellowship as best achieved by poetic, rather than institutional means. Wordsworth's view of human dignity remains revolutionary; but his "rustic poetics" of everyday life represent a radically different way to establish egalitarian conditions, which can restore to humans their lost sense of dignity, alter human sympathy, and ultimately effect a great social transformation.

Wordsworth's hopes for social transformation become evident when read in the context of other, contemporary writings, particularly his letter to the British civil servant Charles James Fox.* In this letter, Wordsworth criticizes the political and economic changes of the late eighteenth century, which, he argues, have resulted in "a rapid decay of the domestic affections among the lower orders of society."[4] This letter to Fox was accompanied by a copy of *Lyrical Ballads,* with its newly installed Preface, and its political passions are carefully integrated with the poetic concerns of the Preface. For Wordsworth, poetry and politics were ultimately inseparable.[5]

Overlooked

Wordsworth's vision of the complementarity of poetic and scientific knowledge is somewhat analogous to the relationship between the humanities and the sciences in the twenty-first century university. Most institutions offer courses in both the humanities and the sciences. Most find a way to acknowledge that the sciences teach students about the principles and processes that govern the behavior of the natural world, including human biology; and also, that the humanities teach students how to think critically, how to analyze ethical and philosophical problems, and how to appreciate and recognize the ways that humans, as individuals and as communities, find meaning and moral value in existence. To many students and teachers of the humanities, it seems obvious that the knowledge gained through the study of literature, religion, history, and philosophy is more important; to students and teachers of the sciences, it seems evident that the knowledge found through human biology, or even through astrophysics, is far more useful to human flourishing. Yet most universities affirm in their course offerings that *both* kinds of knowledge should be part of an undergraduate curriculum. Wordsworth's vision of complementarity is similar. His preference, unsurprisingly, is for the humanities; yet he sees scientific knowledge as critical to the goal of enriching human sympathy, the pleasure found in the natural world, and the depths of human imagination.

In the twenty-first century, few readers would look to Wordsworth as an expert on the subject of the complementarity of scientific and poetic knowledge. The revelations and applications of modern science are so wide-ranging that Wordsworth's delimitations of scientific knowledge are hard to read as anything but extremely outdated. Yet Wordsworth's sense of these two approaches is not entirely inconsistent with the university's contemporary instinct toward complementarity.

This recognition may be helpful for contemporary readers who might otherwise tend to read Wordsworth as a merely nostalgic poet.

The role of science in Wordsworth's thinking about his craft allows us to read *Lyrical Ballads* in a way that might seem to be in opposition to the poems' apparently simple diction and self-conscious appropriation of traditional forms such as the ballad. By following Wordsworth's suggestion, we can recover some of the ways in which this poetry attempted to make itself fit for modernity, rather than turning away from it. By paying proper attention to this aspect of Wordsworth's account of his poetics, we can recover his poetry—and Romantic poetry more generally—from the popular misconception that it is exclusively interested in intense, subjective feeling, rather than in the capacity of language to communicate knowledge.

NOTES

1   William Wordsworth, "Preface" *Lyrical Ballads: 1798 and 1802*, ed. Fiona Stafford (Oxford: Oxford University Press, 2013), 99.

2   Wordsworth, "Preface" *Lyrical Ballads: 1798 and 1802,* 106.

3   Wordsworth, "Preface" *Lyrical Ballads: 1798 and 1802*, 107.

4   William Wordsworth, Letter to Charles James Fox, January 14, 1801. *Lyrical Ballads: 1798 and 1802*, ed. Fiona Stafford (Oxford: Oxford University Press, 2013), 307.

5   Fiona Stafford, "Introduction," *Lyrical Ballads: 1798 and 1802.* William Wordsworth and Samuel Coleridge, ed. Fiona Stafford (Oxford: Oxford University Press, 2013), ··▲··.

MODULE 7
ACHIEVEMENT

KEY POINTS

- The new movement that Wordsworth announced in the Preface is generally seen as having changed poetry in English.

- The popularity of *Lyrical Ballads* contributed powerfully to the success of the Preface.

- The importance of Wordsworth's political and social context in shaping the ideas of the Preface has not always been taken seriously.

Assessing the Argument

The Preface first appeared as an extended introduction to the second edition of *Lyrical Ballads* (1800). The further expansion of the Preface in 1802, and the addition of an appendix on poetic diction, represents a more complete articulation of Wordsworth's conception of the poet, poetic language, and the poet's relationship to society. Throughout this period, *Lyrical Ballads* enjoyed a wide readership and was subject to both intense criticism and superlative acclaim.

If the goal of the Preface had been simply to help readers appreciate the poems collected in *Lyrical Ballads,* it would be hard to argue that the Preface was fully successful; many readers remained puzzled and dissatisfied, and many critics argued fervently against Wordsworth's experiment and the "rustic poetics" he proposed. However, the Preface must be understood to have a broader aspiration, and a more long-term program. Put modestly, Wordsworth's goal was to change the conversation about poetry; this

> ❝ I firmly believe that the poetical performance of Wordsworth is, after that of Shakespeare and Milton, of which all the world now recognizes the worth, undoubtedly the most considerable in our language from the Elizabethan age to the present time. Chaucer is anterior; and on other grounds, too, he cannot well be brought into the comparison. But taking the roll of our chief poetical names, besides Shakespeare and Milton...I think it certain that Wordsworth's name deserves to stand, and will finally stand, above them all. Several of the poets named have gifts and excellences which Wordsworth has not. But taking the performance of each as a whole, I say that Wordsworth seems to me to have left a body of poetical work superior in power, in interest, in the qualities which give enduring freshness, to that which any one of the others has left. ❞
>
> Matthew Arnold, "Wordsworth"

he certainly achieved. Put more grandly, Wordsworth intended to change poetry in English forever; and most critics now agree that Wordsworth *did* ultimately revolutionize poetry. Along with Coleridge, Wordsworth is generally recognized as having inaugurated the Romantic movement in literature. The Preface is not solely responsible for the success of Wordsworth's new poetics; without the *Lyrical Ballads* themselves, which captivated and provoked readers on their own, the proclamations of the Preface might have been entirely forgotten. But it is indisputable that Wordsworth's Preface contributed powerfully to his campaign for a poetic revolution.

Achievement in Context

The Preface was persuasive in large part because of the popularity of the *Lyrical Ballads* that it was explicitly intended to defend. Many of those who had read the first edition of the *Ballads* in 1798 were eager to read the 1800 Preface to see what more Wordsworth had to say about these experimental poems. Some readers had responded to the *Ballads* with a mixture of curiosity and apprehension; others had been caught up in the vision of the *Ballads* and now hoped to be a part of the movement that Wordsworth had announced. The 1800 Preface also made enough of a splash in London literary circles that it broadened the readership of the *Ballads*; because of the Preface, some readers found themselves reading the *Ballads* in 1800 for the first time. The relationship between the poems and the Preface became powerfully symbiotic. For many critics, the poems of *Lyrical Ballads* were evidence of Wordsworth's prescience; if they liked the poems, they were likely to be persuaded that the Preface's manifesto represented a bright future for poetry. Whether they read the poems first, and then the Preface, or the other way around—and whether they responded with zeal or repugnance—most readers were able to recognize that Wordsworth was doing something radically new.

Limitations

The Preface to *Lyrical Ballads* turns on the idea of permanence. It seeks to establish a language that is rooted in human nature, and which is at its most visible and most enduring in "rustic" forms of life. Wordsworth argues at the beginning of his Preface that if those suggestions that he makes in it "were indeed realized, a class of Poetry would be produced, well adapted to interest mankind permanently."[1] That insistence on permanence is itself a product of its time, especially Wordsworth's own experience of great social changes of the late eighteenth century. By the time he wrote the Preface, Britain had experienced a rapid depopulation of rural communities, expedited by the Industrial Revolution; Britain was also in the middle of a protracted war with France, and Europe had been shaken by the French Revolution and the subsequent "Terror," which Wordsworth himself had narrowly escaped.

Wordsworth makes little explicit reference to these social, historical, and personal uncertainties in the text itself. However, it is precisely at the point of his insistence on the value of permanence that this uncertainty, and Wordsworth's reaction to it, becomes visible: his insistence on permanence is itself a reaction to, and an attempt to establish a corrective to, prevailing uncertainty. Wordsworth's location of this permanence in figures and customs of laboring classes, rural life, and the natural world was itself a radical gesture, indicating the shared humanity of all classes, in all times and places.

Criticism of the text has often focused on Wordsworth's understanding of permanence as vested in rural life, which Wordsworth saw as exemplifying the changelessness of the natural world and of human passions. For Victorian thinkers such as J.S. Mill* and Matthew Arnold,* the terms set out in the Preface offer an account of social relations and of art's function within those relations that served as a counterpoint to the materialism of the new century; Wordsworth's concerns about the effect of increasing urbanization also seemed powerfully shaped by the culture of Britain at the turn of the century. This culturally specific reading has occasionally contributed to the perception of Wordsworth as a poet advocating a celebration of nature as an escape from political and social challenges. But to focus exclusively on Wordsworth's dedication to nature and solitude is often to miss the democratic political commitments that powerfully shaped his poetics and his ideology.

In its conception of the relationship between society and nature, the Preface to *Lyrical Ballads* has exerted influence beyond the boundaries of poetics and literary criticism. This has particularly been the case with regard to the Preface's celebration of "rustic" life and language, which has been understood as a call radically to reevaluate the economic and social order of an increasingly industrialized society. The Preface thus articulates a principle that would become central to Romantic thought and art, that nature and the natural world are the source and substance of the imagination and of human sympathy. Wordsworth's articulation of the incursions being made on the sacred space of the natural by the processes of industrialization and urbanization is the definitive statement of this position.

NOTES

1   William Wordsworth, "Preface" *Lyrical Ballads: 1798 and 1802*, ed. Fiona Stafford (Oxford: Oxford University Press, 2013), 95.

MODULE 8
PLACE IN THE AUTHOR'S WORK

KEY POINTS

- The Preface was written in the first years of Wordsworth's "great decade" (1798-1807).

- Wordsworth continued to revise the Preface and to republish his early poems for the rest of his life.

- The Preface is one of the most influential documents of literary criticism in English.

Positioning

Wordsworth wrote the Preface to *Lyrical Ballads* at the age of 30. *Lyrical Ballads* contains the first work that anticipates Wordsworth's mature style: most of his earlier work was not included in *Lyrical Ballads*, though "The Female Vagrant" is an exception. Wordsworth lived for another half century after the first publication of the Preface, and he continued to write and to publish poetry, though with less frequency, for many of those years. The Preface and the *Lyrical Ballads* themselves, written so early in his career, are nonetheless regarded as among his greatest works, exemplifying and clarifying the poetic vision to which his entire career was dedicated.

In the years between 1797 and 1807, Wordsworth wrote, or began to write, most of the poems for which he is best known. Along with *Lyrical Ballads,* the Preface marks the beginning of what scholars often call his "great decade," and the works that followed over the course of the next seven years represent Wordsworth's greatest period of creativity and experimentation. He continued to make changes to the Preface and to revise his poems for the rest of his life, although the amendments after 1802 were far slighter than the changes between

> **❝** If there be one conclusion more forcibly pressed upon us than another by the review which has been given of the fortunes and fate of poetical Works, it is this—that every author, as far as he is great and at the same time *original*, has had the task of *creating* the taste by which he is to be enjoyed: so has it been, so will it continue to be. **❞**
>
> Wordsworth, "Essay, Supplementary to the Preface," *Poems, 1815*

1798 and 1802. Most contemporary critics have agreed that the later changes to the Preface are of marginal importance to an understanding of the work's importance, and that the 1802 version most fully and accurately articulates Wordsworth's vision of poetic language and the true poetic character.

The Preface, the *Lyrical Ballads,* and several other poems that Wordsworth wrote between 1800 and 1807 together make up the work for which Wordsworth is best known: the *Prelude* (1804–1805) and *Ode: Intimations of Immortality* (1804) were also written during this period, rounding out the short list of works that remain popular subjects of study and discussion today.

Integration

Even after this decade, however, Wordsworth's revisions of the Preface and of the poems in *Lyrical Ballads* constituted a significant part of the work that would occupy him for the rest of his career. The ideas expressed in the Preface shifted slightly as it underwent these revisions, resulting in occasional contradictions. It is difficult, for instance, to reconcile the celebration of "rustic" forms of language and life from the 1800 Preface with the 1802 insertion that emphasizes the poet's role in selecting and refining "the language really spoken by men ... with true feeling," so that it might "form a distinction far greater than would at first be imagined, and will entirely separate the composition from the vulgarity and meanness of ordinary life."[1] On the one hand, Wordsworth seems to advocate the glories of the "ordinary"; on the other, he claims to have sifted out everything "ordinary" in the creative process. These contradictions often mark changes in Wordsworth's thinking that have not yet been fully harmonized with the rest of his arguments in the Preface.

Despite the confusions that occasionally resulted from Wordsworth's revisions, the arguments of the Preface remained largely cohesive: Wordsworth's celebration of a "rustic poetics" emphasized the beauty of the natural world and of the human sympathy found in everyday rural life (even as it criticized the conditions of everyday life in urban centers), and the special role of the poet in revealing beauty and sympathy. On the whole, ideological inconsistencies between the various versions of the Preface are minor. Together, they can be read as documenting the development of Wordsworth's mind and work over the course of his career, rather than as a straightforward presentation of fully formed convictions. As an attempt to articulate the credos underpinning the poems of *Lyrical Ballads*, the Preface succeeds in what it set out to do; its poetic and social principles became the basis for the aesthetic and ethical commitments of Romanticism, which became the major literary movement of the nineteenth century.

Significance

It is difficult to underestimate the importance of the Preface. It has remained in print, and been studied and discussed for more than two centuries. The history of its reception has been marked by controversy as well as endurance. Even Wordsworth and Coleridge sought within their lifetimes to distance themselves from aspects of it (Wordsworth in his "Essay, Supplementary to the Preface" of 1815, and Coleridge in *Biographia Literaria* in 1817). Later Romantic poets such as Lord Byron* ridiculed the earnestness of the Preface and Wordsworth's other prose additions, opening his own Preface to *Don Juan* by questioning the intelligibility of these earlier works. A century later, when T.S. Eliot* composed his own seminal work on the art of poetry, "Tradition and the Individual Talent," he, too, cited Wordsworth's Preface as a point of departure. It is a testament to the importance and influence of the Preface to *Lyrical Ballads* that these later poets framed their own poetic ideas and identities directly in relation to Wordsworth's thinking in the Preface.

For the Victorian critic Matthew Arnold, the terms of the Preface returned its readers to the "joy offered to us in nature, the joy offered to us in the simple, primary affections and duties."[2] Arnold's insistence on the alignment of the natural with the moral in Wordsworth exemplifies the Victorians' reading of Wordsworth's work and life, which found in Wordsworth's poetry a sense of the natural world and its implicit order, in contrast to the rapid industrialization of the nineteenth century and its dislocating effect on society. Arnold's interpretation of the Preface and of Wordsworth's work broadly was extremely influential on readings of Wordsworth in the nineteenth and early twentieth centuries. With the publication of the Preface and the second edition of *Lyrical Ballads*, Wordsworth presented himself to the literary world as introducing a "rustic" poetics and taking up common, everyday themes. Arnold presented Wordsworth as a poet of nature, and that description has endured.

The conception of Wordsworth as a nature poet was also fortified by Wordsworth's own later work and activism. Famously, he campaigned against the extension of a train line into the Lake District in the 1840s. He lent the full weight of his reputation as Poet Laureate to the cause, writing letters to politicians and influential dignitaries to establish the case against it. "As for holiday pastimes, if a scene is to be chosen suitable to them for persons thronging at a distance," he wrote, "it may be found elsewhere at less cost of every kind."[3] His prose work *Guide to the Lakes* (1822), a sort of tourist guidebook that remains popular among British readers even today, continues to reinforce this reputation. As such, Wordsworth's ideas exerted considerable influence beyond the field of poetry. The popular notion of Wordsworth as a nature poet is not inaccurate, though it tends to abbreviate the complexity of Wordsworth's ideas in the Preface and the populist commitments that animated his thinking and his creative process.

NOTES

1   William Wordsworth, "Preface" *Lyrical Ballads: 1798 and 1802*, ed. Fiona Stafford (Oxford: Oxford University Press, 2013), 102–03.

2   Matthew Arnold, *Lyrical Ballads: A Casebook*, ed. Alun Richard Jones and William Tydeman, (London: Macmillan, 1972), 71.

3   William Wordsworth, *Wordsworth's Guide to the Lakes*, ed. Ernest de Selincourt, (Oxford: Oxford University Press, 1970), 166.

SECTION 3
IMPACT

MODULE 9
THE FIRST RESPONSES

KEY POINTS

- Some of the Preface's critics preferred Wordsworth's poems to his prose.

- Wordsworth's elevation of the role of the poet in the 1802 Preface was partly a response to criticisms of the 1800 Preface.

- Wordsworth's shifting political affiliations made him a controversial figure among the next generation of Romantic poets.

Criticism

The Preface, first published with the second edition of *Lyrical Ballads* in 1800, was itself a response to criticisms of the first edition of *Lyrical Ballads*. The collection was the result of a collaboration between Wordsworth and Samuel Taylor Coleridge, but it was originally published anonymously, with only a brief "Advertisement" included by way of explanation. Despite their enigmatic presentation, these poems met with wide critical appreciation, praised for their beauty, simplicity, and taste. The first edition sold out, which itself was reason to begin work on a second. At the same time, however, some prominent critics had confessed perplexity about these poems, and concern about their implicit politics. Coleridge's *The Rime of the Ancient Mariner,* today perhaps the most famous of the *Lyrical Ballads,* was criticized by Coleridge's own brother-in-law Robert Southey* as "unintelligible," and the collection on the whole, Southey wrote, was "uninteresting." The critic Francis Jeffrey* made similarly scathing criticisms. It must be added that even these critics, who reviewed the *Ballads* more

❝ By 1802, Wordsworth had come to understand that being a 'poet' was not a question of getting published and receiving favourable reviews, but of possessing a certain cast of mind and a heart open to the astonishing revelations of an ordinary day... ❞

Fiona Stafford, "Introduction" to *Lyrical Ballads, 1798 and 1802*

harshly than most, were also known to have found the poems fairly absorbing: Southey included his copy among the few books he took on a long sea voyage in 1800, and Jeffrey admitted to being "enchanted."[1]

When the Preface appeared with the 1800 edition, it was thus already engaged with criticisms of the *Lyrical Ballads* as incoherent, politically radical, and confusing. These early criticisms did not entirely fade with the appearance of the Preface, and the Preface itself was not initially received as warmly as the *Ballads* it set out to defend. The poet and critic Charles Lamb* was receptive to the literary ideas of the Preface, but found his enjoyment occasionally diminished by this lengthy prose explanation. Wordsworth had sent the Preface to the Whig* statesman Charles James Fox along with a letter explaining the political vision of the poems; but in his reply, Fox suggested that the simplicity of Wordsworth's rustic poetry might best be kept separate from the difficulties of political reform. The lofty ambitions of the Preface did not immediately seem promising.

Responses

Wordsworth's 1802 revision of the Preface, like its original composition, was probably in part motivated by the mixed responses of critics; no writer can be totally immune to either acclaim or attack. But the revisions that appeared in 1802 nonetheless proclaimed a kind of immunity from popular review: it was at this stage that Wordsworth introduce his theory of the poet, whose task it was to introduce human delight and to contemplate and celebrate the passions and the very essence of human nature. According to Wordsworth's new theory, the poet had no particular duty to please the great literary minds of his day; the poet's duty, instead, was to humanity itself. In that sense, perhaps Wordsworth's most important response to criticisms of the Preface was his 1802 declaration of the poet's *independence* from criticism.

Perhaps the most important dissenter to the vision of the Preface, as it unfolded in new revisions, was Samuel Taylor Coleridge. Coleridge's relationship to the Preface itself was complicated: though he had no hand in writing it, he and Wordsworth both confirmed that it was largely a product of their friendship and the literary ideals they explored in the course of many conversations and collaborations in their years of friendship. Coleridge nonetheless voiced reservations about it in an 1802 letter to Robert Southey: "Far from going all lengths with Wordsworth," he wrote with respect to the conclusions of the Preface, "I rather suspect that some where or other there is a radical Difference in our theoretical opinions respecting Poetry."[2] This diffidence toward the Preface marks the beginning of Coleridge's gradual distancing of himself from its ideas, and of a growing rift between the two writers, in friendship and in literary ideals.

Conflict and Consensus

Wordsworth's lifelong revisions and republications of the Preface and of *Lyrical Ballads* are testament to his enduring dedication to the principles of these youthful projects. However, Wordsworth's life also demonstrates a gradual drift toward more institutionalist, more conservative affiliations. In 1813 he accepted a government post in the revenue service as Distributor of Stamps for Westmorland; in 1818 he campaigned for an aristocratic Tory* candidate, Lord Lonsdale, with whom he had become intimate; in the 1830s, he opposed new taxes that would threaten the incomes of landowners, as well as systematized welfare policies; and eventually became a vocal defender of Anglicanism.*[3]

By this time, a younger generation of British poets had emerged who shared, in various ways, the poetic vision that Wordsworth had articulated in the Preface. Emphasizing the power of human feeling and experience, the resilience of the imagination, and the beauty of nature and art, these poets are generally hailed as evidence of the new movement he had announced, though many of them expressed strong disagreement with his work or even personal dislike. Like Wordsworth in his youth, the major figures of this movement—known as Romanticism—generally affiliated themselves with the politics of the left. But as Wordsworth began to ally himself with more conservative issues, the new generation of Romantic poets were frequently disappointed by their forebear, not least because of his perceived political defection. When Keats* went to visit Wordsworth in the Lakes, he was disappointed to find that this former supporter of the Revolution was out canvassing for the local Tory* candidate. In her journal, Mary Godwin (not yet Shelley)* records her reaction to Wordsworth's *The Excursion* (1814): "much disappointed—He is a slave…"[4] Perhaps the most savage critic of the first generation of Romantic poets was Lord Byron. His criticism of the Preface suggests that Wordsworth's need to establish the precepts of his poetry indicated his inflated sense of personal authority and of his dedication to marshalling poetry to his own, increasingly conservative, poetics. Byron's description of Wordsworth's "system of prosaic raving"[5] has much in common with earlier criticisms of Wordsworth's everyday subjects in *Lyrical Ballads* and of the prose argument in defense of those poems in the Preface. This attack perhaps also represents Byron's effort to develop his own distinctive voice, both in Wordsworth's wake and in contradistinction to the great poet.

NOTES

1   Fiona Stafford, "Introduction" *Lyrical Ballads: 1798 and 1802,* William Wordsworth and Samuel Coleridge, ed. Fiona Stafford (Oxford: Oxford University Press, 2013), ⋯.

2   Samuel Taylor Coleridge to Robert Southey, July 29, 1802, *Collected Letters, 1801-1806*, Volume II, ed. Earl Leslie Griggs (Oxford: Oxford University Press, 2002), 830.

3   Nicola Trott, "Wordsworth: the shape of the poetic career," in *The Cambridge Companion to Wordsworth,* ed. Stephen Gill (Cambridge: Cambridge University Press, 2003), 6.

4   Mary Wollstonecraft Shelley, September 14, 1814, *The Journals of Mary Shelley: Volume 2, 1814-1844*, ed. Paula Feldman and Diana Scott-Kilvert (Oxford: Oxford University Press, 1987), 25.

5   Lord Byron, "Dedication," in *Don Juan*, ed. T. G. Steffan, E. Steffan and W. W. Pratt (London: Penguin, 2004), 42.

MODULE 10
THE EVOLVING DEBATE

KEY POINTS

- In the years after the Preface appeared, Coleridge distanced himself from Wordsworth's ideas.

- Some of the greatest figures of the nineteenth century, both within literature and beyond it, said that they were indebted to the Preface.

- Poets writing in English have continually turned to the Preface to define their own poetic ideals.

Uses and Problems

The projects Wordsworth undertook after 1807 are generally thought to mark something of a decline in his poetic output. The style of *The Excursion* (1814), perhaps the best-known poem of his later career, is ponderous and abstruse when compared with the moving immanence and immediacy of *The Prelude* (1799-1805). The Preface to the *Poems, 1815,* and the "Essay, Supplementary to the Preface," articulate a different set of preoccupations from those in the 1802 Preface. The focus on "the real language of men" in the earlier work is replaced by a more technical discussion of the differences between creative "fancy" and "imagination"; and the "rustic" forms of society valorized in the 1802 Preface have been replaced with a more broadly conceptualized "Public."[1]

In particular, Wordsworth states that "fancy," like imagination, can be a creative faculty, in direct contradiction of Coleridge's assertion that fancy is necessarily distinct from imagination. Wordsworth's conflation of the two particularly irritated Coleridge, who saw a clear distinction between them: this disagreement spurred him finally to

> ❝ To [the Preface] I reply; that a rustic's language, purified from all provincialism and grossness, and so far re-constructed as to be made consistent with the rules of grammar—(which are in essence no other than the laws of universal logic, applied to psychological materials)—will not differ from the language of any other man of common sense, however learned or refined he may be, except as far as the notions, which the rustic has to convey, are fewer and more indiscriminate... ❞
>
> Samuel Taylor Coleridge, *Biographia Literaria*

begin the composition of *Biographia Literaria,* his own account of poetry and poetics. Published in 1817, the *Biographia* reflects extensively on the composition of *Lyrical Ballads*, and engages in a sustained rebuttal of the central tenets of the Preface. Coleridge reserves his criticism in particular for Wordsworth's privileging of rustic life and language, stating that this language "will not differ from the language of any other man of common sense, however learned or refined he may be, except as far as the notions, which the rustic has to convey, are fewer and more indiscriminate."[2] Coleridge's somewhat aristocratic defense of erudition and refinement in part reflects his turn toward philosophical work and his increasing engagement as a lecturer at universities across Britain. Among scholars of Romanticism and of nineteenth century thought, *Biographia Literaria* is generally regarded as more coherent and more philosophically complex than the *Preface.* However, as a manifesto of Romantic poets, the Preface remained the primary document with which poets of the nineteenth and even the early twentieth century would struggle in their own quests to define their literary voices.

Schools of Thought

The Preface continued to exert considerable influence after Wordsworth's death, including in disciplines beyond poetry. Some of the greatest British minds of the nineteenth century described various personal and artistic debts to the Preface. The novelist George Eliot* drew on its example when she described realism* as "the doctrine that all truth and beauty are to be attained by a humble and faithful study of nature."[3] In his *Autobiography*, J.S. Mill recalls how reading Wordsworth was a key moment in his own recovery from his depression. "What made Wordsworth's poems a medicine for my state of mind," Mill writes, "was that they expressed, not mere outward beauty, but states of feeling, and of thought colored by feeling, under the excitement of beauty..."[4] Mill's account of Wordsworth's poetry functioning as a spiritual palliative or remedy contributed to Wordsworth's reputation and readership throughout the nineteenth century.

The Preface's realist strain also had practical implications: the Wordsworth Society, founded in 1880, sought to preserve both Wordsworth's manuscripts and, in John Ruskin's* words, "the conditions of rural life which made Wordsworth himself possible."[5] This preservation took the form of campaigning on issues affecting the Lake District in particular, continuing Wordsworth's own opposition to the incursion of the railways, for example. It is worth noting that such campaigns engaged more with the Preface as a forerunner of such later writings as *A Guide Through the District of the Lakes in the North of England* (1835), which focuses more on the rural as an idyll rather than as the site of economic and political tensions that Wordsworth celebrated in *Lyrical Ballads.* The Preface's insistence on the common bond of humanity that transcended social hierarchies also became a point of reference for the various socialist* movements that rose up in England in the 1880s.

A different critical perspective began to emerge at the turn of the twentieth century. T.S. Eliot expressly disagreed with Wordsworth's definition of poetry as "emotion recollected in tranquility," arguing that poetry was a disciplined process that was ultimately an escape from emotion and personality. Eliot's criticisms of Wordsworth and of Romanticism exercised a powerful influence on Anglophone poetry, contributing to the rise of the New Criticism* and of Formalist* schools of poetry that dominated British and American letters in the middle of the twentieth century.

In Current Scholarship

The Irish poet Seamus Heaney*—in style and subject an extremely Wordsworthian writer—argued in 2006 that Wordsworth remains "an indispensable figure in the evolution of modern writing, a finder-and-keeper of the self-as-subject, a theorist and apologist whose Preface to *Lyrical Ballads* remains definitive."[6] It is also worth noting the importance of Wordsworth to contemporary poets writing in a very different tradition to Heaney. The poet J.H. Prynne,* whose work is marked by an experimental and highly self-conscious style, wrote a recent critical study and has lectured on Wordsworth extensively at the University of Cambridge. Wordsworth's importance to both of these two drastically different poets is a testament to the enduring power of his corpus and of the literary ideals announced in the Preface.

Current proponents of Wordsworth's Preface to *Lyrical Ballads* engage with a number of different aspects of the text. For example, for literary scholars working in an ecocritical* tradition, aspects of the claims made by Wordsworth in the Preface resonate with their ecological concerns. This is particularly the case with Wordsworth's comments about the negative effects of urbanization—a process that was just beginning as Wordsworth wrote the *Preface*, and has since then contributed to major population shifts all over the world. Wordsworth's environmentalism thus reads like something of a prophecy fulfilled. The *Preface* and Wordsworth's work more generally is the subject of one of the earliest and most famous articulations of ecocriticism, Jonathan Bate's* *Romantic Ecology* (1991). This body of work has generally represented accurately the Preface's principled criticisms of urbanization, and its dedication to the natural world; however, its emphasis on these aspects has somewhat overshadowed the more explicitly political tensions in the work. As such, ecocritical work has occasionally oversimplified the Preface, ignoring the political concerns that lie just beneath its surface.

NOTES

1   William Wordsworth, "Preface" to *Poems*, 1815. *William Wordsworth: The Major Works*, ed. Stephen Gill (Oxford: Oxford University Press, 2000), 626–39.

2   Samuel Taylor Coleridge, *Biographia Literaria*, in *The Major Works*, ed. H.J. Jackson (Oxford: Oxford University Press, 2000 [1817]), 341.

3   George Eliot (1991 [1856]), 368.

4   J. S. Mill, *Autobiography* (London: Penguin Classics, 1989), 116.

5   John Ruskin to William Knight, April 3, 1883. Quoted in Stephen Gill, *Wordsworth and the Victorians* (Oxford: Oxford University Press, 1998), 246.

6   Seamus Heaney, "The Triumph of Spirit," *Guardian,* February 11, 2006.

MODULE 11
IMPACT AND INFLUENCE TODAY

KEY POINTS

- Wordsworth's enduring influence can be observed in the popularity of his work on college and university syllabi and among literary scholars.
- Humanist interpretations dominated Wordsworth studies in the middle of the twentieth century.
- Historical studies now represent the primary scholarly approach to Wordsworth's work.

Position

Wordsworth's contemporary relevance can be best understood by the attention that his work receives from literary scholars. In English departments in both the United Kingdom and the United States, Wordsworth is still regarded as one of the greatest British writers, a peer to such literary giants as Shakespeare and Milton. Scholars of English literature remain passionately concerned with the interpretation of Wordsworth's work, with his role in the Romanticism movement, and with the way his work anticipates the aesthetics and the ethical preoccupations of twentieth and twenty-first century poetry. The question of what Wordsworth's work means—both individual works, and his corpus on the whole—remains a subject of constant debate. As central projects of Wordsworth's "great decade" (1798-1807), *Lyrical Ballads* and the Preface are primary subjects of that debate.

In the second half of the twentieth century, the dominant critical position on *Lyrical Ballads* was that of Harold Bloom* and Lionel Trilling.* They described Wordsworth as belonging to a "High

> ❝ Wordsworth thus holds a position in the history
> of criticism which must be called ambiguous or
> transitional. He inherited from neo-classicism a theory
> of the imitation of nature to which he gives, however,
> a specific social twist: he inherited from the eighteenth
> century a view of poetry as passion and emotion which
> he again modified as ... 'recollection in tranquility.' He
> takes up rhetorical ideas about the effect of poetry but
> extends and amplifies them into a theory of the social
> effects of literature ... he also adopts a theory of poetry
> in which imagination holds the central place as a power
> of unification and ultimate insight into the unity of the
> world. Though Wordsworth left only a small body of
> criticism, it is rich in survivals, suggestions, anticipations
> and personal insights. ❞
>
> Rene Wellek, *A History of Modern Criticism*

Romantic" moment, which they define in terms of the individual poet's internal "realization of the Sublime." In other words, Bloom and Trilling saw Wordsworth as the great poet of interiority, who pushed Romanticism to its limits by situating heroic drama in the imagination of the poet.[1] Their account, sometimes described as a "humanist" account because of its emphasis on individual imaginative power, prioritizes the personal subject, the ego, and the individual's artistic and intellectual journey. By comparison, in this account social or historical factors are regarded as relatively unimportant to an understanding of Wordsworth's work. Such an account of Romanticism prioritizes those aspects of the Preface to *Lyrical Ballads* that insist on the primacy of the poet and his experience.

A great deal of work has been done since to question this reading of Romanticism. Much of this work has attempted to recover the historical and social concerns of Wordsworth's work, and of Romanticism more broadly, for which Bloom and Trilling's reading fails to account. Jerome McGann's* *The Romantic Ideology* is a significant moment in the development of a prevailing counter-reading to Bloom and Trilling. McGann's argument deconstructs the subjectivity at the center of Bloom and Trilling's argument, aiming instead to ground Wordsworth's work, along with other major artefacts of literary Romanticism, in social-historical analysis. In McGann's exposition, Wordsworth's work is shown to be deliberately ideological; its dream visions have a beginning and ending point in historical time; its imaginative wanderings are not an escape from history and culture, but a revelation that is tempered by its historical context. In particular McGann cites the Preface to the *Lyrical Ballads* as revealing its cultural and historical situation in the strong distinction it makes between the truths of poetry and those of science.[2]

Interaction

The movement away from the humanist consensus evinced by famous critics of the mid-twentieth century such as Harold Bloom and Lionel Trilling has taken a number of different forms. McGann's cultural-historicist* work to place the works of Romanticism within their social and historical framework represents a particularly important contribution, one that opened the door to more many social, ethical and pragmatic programs of interpreting Wordsworth's work. One such program is ecocriticism,* which has sought to establish Romantic literary works within a tradition that is at once intellectual and pragmatic, arguing that these works were engaged with ecological concerns at the time of their composition and that this engagement guarantees their continued relevance to the present day. Robert Mayo offers another approach, situating the poems and

Preface not in a discourse privileging the difficulties of individual genius but rather within the prevailing social context of changing labor practices and conditions.

Simon Jarvis's* more recent intervention in this debate explores the ways in which Wordsworth's philosophical intentions for his work are realized in the poetry itself, rather than in the standard prose language of intellectual debate. For Jarvis, Wordsworth's poetry must be understood as exploring the process and philosophy of creativity, rather than as the working out of higher philosophical ideals that would be more clearly expressed in prose. This reading of Wordsworth on the one hand emphasizes the high value of the poems over such explanatory prose works as the Preface. But at the same time, Jarvis often turns to the Preface as the articulation of Wordsworth's high view of poetry itself, and in particular to the Preface's insistence that poetry is "the breath and finer spirit of all knowledge."[3] in Jarvis's account, this knowledge is contained in the movement of the breath and spirit in the moment of the poetry's reading. Thus, even as scholarly attention has returned to the poems themselves, the Preface remains an essential point of reference for understanding Wordsworth's sense of his own work.

The Continuing Debate

Lyrical Ballads and Wordsworth's work more broadly have been central to the development of ecocriticism; one of the foundational texts of this movement, Jonathan Bate's *Romantic Ecology* (1991), takes Wordsworth as its subject. The book argues for the contemporary importance of reading Wordsworth and other Romantic writers as ecological thinkers, citing their concerns for the integrity of the natural world and their skepticism toward the emerging imperatives of economic growth and material production. Bate argues that the environmental revelations and disasters of the late twentieth and early twenty-first century make Wordsworth's work more important than ever. Along with the works of his fellow Romantic writers, Wordsworth's corpus bears on "what are likely to be some of the most pressing political issues of the coming decade: the greenhouse effect and the depletion of the ozone layer, the destruction of the tropical rainforest, acid rain, the pollution of the sea, and, more locally, the concreting of England's green and pleasant land."[4] Bate's work is almost thirty years old, and the depletions of natural resources and prospect of dangerous climate change now sound somewhat dated. In its suggestion that environmentalism is the new Marxism,* *Romantic Ecology* also exposes what some thinkers regard as an ex-Marxist fallacy, that is, the notion that Marxism became irrelevant with the collapse of the Soviet Union and the fall of the Berlin Wall.* Bate's sense of having moved beyond Marxism as a school of thought sounds premature, especially in the light of the near collapse of the global banking system in 2008. Nonetheless, Bate set an important precedent for reading Wordsworth that considers not only the historical context, but also the ethical and social mandates of his work.

NOTES

1   Harold Bloom and Lionel Trilling, *Romantic Prose and Poetry* (Oxford: Oxford University Press, 1973), 6.

2   Jerome McGann, *The Romantic Ideology: A Critical Investigation* (Chicago: University of Chicago Press, 1985), 69–70.

3   William Wordsworth, "Preface" *Lyrical Ballads: 1798 and 1802*, ed. Fiona Stafford (Oxford: Oxford University Press, 2013), 106.

4   Jonathan Bate, *Romantic Ecology: Wordsworth and the Environmental Tradition* (London: Routledge, 1991), 9.

MODULE 12
WHERE NEXT?

KEY POINTS

- The Preface continues to shed light on contemporary concerns, and to illuminate the historical context in which it was written.

- Historical and cultural analysis of Wordsworth's work has generated many new questions and directions for Wordsworth studies.

- The Preface remains important for understanding modern debates in English literature, including debates over the nature of poetry itself.

Potential

The Preface to *Lyrical Ballads* is a crucial document in the history of English poetry. Part of the Preface's enduring importance is a consequence of its explanatory relationship with the poems in *Lyrical Ballads*, written by one of the greatest English poets at the height of his powers. But likewise, the importance of *Lyrical Ballads* derives in part from the Preface, which offers the fullest articulation of Wordsworth's poetic beliefs at the richest moment of his creative life, and which became the manifesto of the new Romantic movement in poetry at the turn of the twentieth century. In this sense, the Preface is significant as a classic work of literature that explains a distinctive literary ideal, and as a historical document that has exercised great power over British writers, from 1800 to the present. Wordsworth's descriptions of the poetic impulse remain a powerful influence on contemporary understandings of the creative process and of poetry itself. Even as contemporary scholars offer new and compelling interpretations of

> ❝ It is hard, then, to see Wordsworth's theory of balladry [in the Preface and in *Lyrical Ballads*] either as a radically democratic revolution in poetic form or as a retreat from the world of politics into aesthetics. Rather it appears as a careful, complex, at times almost tortured attempt to find a secure place for his collection in the midst of an often divisive debate about how ballads should be valued and understood. ❞
>
> Ian Newman, "Moderation in the *Lyrical Ballads*: Wordsworth and the Ballad Debates of the 1790s"

the Preface that speak to contemporary ethical and artistic concerns, historical analysis of the Preface and its context continues to shed light on the world of eighteenth and nineteenth century Britain. Hence the Preface shows great potential as a source that both inspires readers in the present and informs readers about the past.

Future Directions

As Kenneth Johnston observes, the insights of the Preface into the power of language to shape society and culture, along with human nature itself, are now broadly accepted,[1] if not everywhere associated with Wordsworth. But Wordsworth scholarship increasingly appreciates the Preface's theoretical insights into such issues. Increasingly, the Preface has been appreciated as positioning poetry as the heroic opponent of industrialization and other economic and cultural institutions that threaten the human spirit; this recognition of the Preface's cultural warfare makes the historical context of late eighteenth-century Britain particularly important to the future of Wordsworth scholarship.

As the tide has turned toward historical and cultural analysis of Wordsworth's works, scholars have been increasingly equipped to address historical questions of literary genre as a mode of analyzing the social and linguistic significance of *Lyrical Ballads.* Baron (1995) argued that Wordsworth used local English dialects in the *Ballads* only to imply a regional nature throughout the text, so that the poems might appear "rustic" without alienating a national readership. McEathron (1999), in a similar way, developed an earlier argument made by Mayo (1954) to explore the ways in which *Lyrical Ballads* and the Preface manipulate the tropes of eighteenth-century "peasant poetry" in the service of its aesthetic vision. But Broadhead (2010) has suggested that the language of the *Ballads* is often highly localized, manifesting a deeper, more authentic relationship with dialects than has generally been thought; and that the 1800 *Ballads* and the Preface appeal to the discourses of different literary genres in order, finally, to collapse the distinctions between high and low genres, literary and popular forms, and standard and non-standard English. In 2016 alone, several articles focused on the historical and social significance of *Lyrical Ballads* and the Preface as sites for Wordsworth's engagement with ideas of literary property (Lowe); his response to the politically charged debates about the ballad genre in the 1790s (Newman); and the explorations and representation of social outcasts and human nature (Hall).

While such scholarship offers highly technical literary analysis, it is nonetheless broad in implication. Such scholarship indicates the promise of a possible future direction for Wordsworth scholarship, exploring the extent to which the deeply populist values that Wordsworth claimed were realized in the Preface, and the strength of the *Lyrical Ballads'* revolutionary "democratization" of language. These projects continue to give readers a richer and more complicated picture of who Wordsworth was, of the historical and social factors that shaped his thinking, and of the ways in which the Preface manifests both continuity *and* innovation with these contexts, as they are more clearly understood. In short, the historical turn in Wordsworth studies shows no sign of relenting.

Summary

The importance of the Preface is assured for as long as William Wordsworth retains his reputation as one of the greatest poets in the English language. To students and researchers of British Romanticism, it is a text of paramount importance; to readers of English-language poetry more generally, it remains one of the most compelling and memorable articulations of a poetic credo by a major poet. The Preface has introduced some of the most abiding critical terms in English literature: it is difficult to think of two more celebrated and enduring critical maxims than Wordsworth's definition of poetry as "the spontaneous overflow of powerful feelings ... recollected in tranquillity."[2]

Although the Preface is a product of the specific social and historical context in which it was written, it remains relevant more than 200 years after its composition. To poets writing after Wordsworth, it has been a source text to which they have returned when they have sought to articulate and define a sense of their own poetics: this holds true for poets as culturally and temperamentally different as John Keats and T.S. Eliot. The Preface also remains crucially important to any reading of Wordsworth's work, particularly *Lyrical Ballads* and the work Wordsworth produced during his "great decade" (1798-1807). The critical premises of the Preface allow us to return again and again to the *Ballads'* mixture of simplicity and difficulty with new confidence and energy. But they also continue to provoke debate about the very nature of poetry itself.

NOTES

1   Kenneth R. Johnston, "Wordsworth's Self-Creation and the *1800: Lyrical Ballads*," in *1800: The New Lyrical Ballads*, ed. Nicola Trott and Seamus Perry (Houndmills: Palgrave, 2001), 115.

2   William Wordsworth, "Preface" *Lyrical Ballads: 1798 and 1802*, ed. Fiona Stafford (Oxford: Oxford University Press, 2013), 111.

GLOSSARY

GLOSSARY OF TERMS

Anglicanism: the tradition of Christian religion as practiced in the British Isles since the Reformation. The Church of England broke away from the Catholic Church during the Reformation, and in the era of the British empire, Anglicanism spread globally as the religion of the British colonies. Anglicanism remains the official religious tradition of the United Kingdom.

Berlin Wall: a wall built by communist East Germany that divided East and West Berlin from 1961 to 1989. It was a key symbol of the barrier between communism and democratic capitalism during the Cold War—the state of tension and rivalry between the two camps until the collapse of the communist bloc between 1989 and 1991.

Cultural historicism: a school of critical thought that seeks to analyze texts and events in terms of their original historical context.

Ecocriticism: a late twentieth- and early twenty-first-century school of critical thought that seeks to understand the ecological significance of literary work.

Enlightenment: an intellectual and philosophical movement that dominated European thought and culture in the eighteenth century. The Enlightenment emphasized the value of reason over dogma and tradition, upholding ideals such as liberty, fraternity, and the separation of church and state.

French Revolution: in the French Revolution (1789), the French royal family was deposed by a popular revolt. The revolution espoused the principles of liberty, equality, and fraternity. The early years of Revolution were followed by a period of extreme violence, sometime referred to as "The Terror," in which tens of thousands of French citizens were executed for allegedly opposing the Revolution.

Industrial Revolution: a period of rapid development in industry that took place in England in the late eighteenth and early nineteenth centuries, chiefly owing to the introduction of new or improved machinery and large-scale production methods.

The Lake District: a region in Cumbria, in the north of England, covering 866 square miles and including the largest lakes and highest peaks in England, such as Lake Windermere and Scafell Pike. The region is particularly associated with Wordsworth, who was born in Cumbria, and who returned to make his home there as an adult and celebrate the beauties of the region in poetic and prose works.

Marxism: political and economic theory developed by Karl Marx (1818-83), author of *Capital* and *The Communist Manifesto*. Marx was a German philosopher and economist and the principal theoretician of communism. His theories have been widely employed over time, resulting in many varieties of Marxist thought. It generally involves the belief in an inevitable struggle between classes that either control or labour for the production of goods and in the empowerment of the labour classes to achieve social reform.

The New Criticism: a major school of Anglophone literary scholarship which favored internal methods of reading texts, emphasizing the independence of the text from any biographical or personal influences and its formal and stylistic integrity.

Poetics: the area of literary criticism and theory that deals with poetry, its techniques, its language, and its aesthetics.

Poet Laureate: an honor bestowed for preeminent poetic excellence, usually by the head of state. In Britain, the tradition of a poet laureate dates to the seventeenth century; other nations (such as the United States) have since adopted the practice.

The Quantocks: a range of hills—today designated an Area of Outstanding Natural Beauty—near Bridgwater in Somerset, southwest England.

Realism: an aesthetic movement, most active in the second half of the nineteenth century, that valued accurate portrayals of moods, scenes, and people.

Romanticism: an aesthetic and intellectual movement in the early nineteenth century that emphasized the primacy of subjective experience and the imagination, and of the revelatory power of the natural world. The Romantic movement influenced philosophers, artists, writers, and musicians working across Europe. In this analysis, the term refers specifically to the literary movement in Britain called Romanticism. *Lyrical Ballads* is often seen as one of the first Romantic texts written in Britain.

Socialism: a political and economic system that emphasises cooperation over competition, and mutual rather than private ownership of goods.

Tintern Abbey: a religious house, now in ruins, that lies on the bank of the River Wye in the village of Tintern, Monmouthshire, Wales. The abbey was founded by Walter de Clare, Lord of Chepstow in 1131. The ruins are associated with Wordsworth because of his poem "Lines Written a Few Miles Above Tintern Abbey, on Revisiting the Banks of the Wye on a Tour. July 13, 1798."

Tory: in British political life of the eighteenth and early nineteenth century the two main political factions were Whigs and Tories. By the late eighteenth and early nineteenth century, Tories largely represented the country gentry while Whigs supported reformers and industrialists. Tories are the forerunners of the modern Conservative Party in Britain.

Whig: see "Tory."

PEOPLE MENTIONED IN THE TEXT

Matthew Arnold (1822–1888) was a British poet and critic, addressing literary, social, and cultural issues in his criticism. Writing as he did at the close of the Victorian era and the beginning of the modern, Arnold is now commonly regarded as the most modern, and most sage, of the Victorian writers.

Jonathan Bate (born 1958) is a British writer and literary scholar, specializing in the work of Shakespeare and Wordsworth. He is particularly known for his contributions to the ecocritical school of literary studies. Bate is Professor of English Literature at the University of Oxford.

Harold Bloom (born 1930) is an American literary critic and the Sterling Professor Humanities at Yale University. He is best known for his theory of literary influence, presented in works such as *The Anxiety of Influence (1973), Shakespeare and the Invention of the Human* (1998), and *The Anatomy of Influence* (2011).

Robert Burns (1759-1796) was a poet and farmer. Though well-educated, Burns became the icon of the "primitive" poet idealized in Romantic critical theory. Many of his lyrics were set to music, making lyrics such as "Auld lang syne" and "Flow Gently Sweet Afton" some of the most famous of Romantic poems.

Lord Byron (George Gordon Byron, 1788-1824) was an English poet, author of *Childe Harold's Pilgrimage* and many short poems, and a colorful member of the Romantic generation. In *Don Juan*, a long, brilliantly satirical poem, Byron pokes fun at the ideology of Wordsworth's Preface.

Samuel Taylor Coleridge (1774-1832) was an English poet, critic, and philosopher. Wordsworth's great friend, he was co-author of *Lyrical Ballads*. The *Biographia Literaria* (1817) is Coleridge's philosophical autobiography, in which he also sets out his account of poetic language and a summation of his philosophical convictions.

George Eliot (Mary Ann Evans, 1819-80) was a British novelist and critic. She is best known for her achievements of literary realism in such novels *Middlemarch, Adam Bede,* and *Daniel Deronda.*

T. S. Eliot (1888-1965) was an American-born poet and critic. Best known for such long poems as *The Love Song of J. Alfred Prufrock* and *The Waste Land,* he exerted a powerful influence on the direction of twentieth-century poetry and poetics.

Charles James Fox (1749-1806) was a British politician and promoter of liberty, who served as foreign secretary in 1782, 1783, and 1806.

William Godwin (1756-1836) was an English political thinker and novelist. He is best known for *Political Justice,* an anarchist philosophical response to the French Revolution.

Thomas Gray (1716-71) was an English poet, best known for "Elegy Written in a Country Churchyard."

William Hazlitt (1778-1830) was the preeminent critic of the Romantic generation, known for his intelligent grasp of Romantic literature and art as well for his journalistic essays on a broad range of topics.

Seamus Heaney (1939–2013) was an Irish poet. Known for his celebration of Irish language and culture, he was awarded the Nobel Prize for Literature in 1995.

Horace (Quintus Horatius Flaccus, **65 BCE – 8 BCE)** was a classical Roman poet, known for satiric and lyric verse.

Charles Lamb (1775–1834) was a poet and essayist of the Romantic generation, known for his brilliant sociability as much as for his mastery of the personal essay.

Simon Jarvis (born 1963) is a contemporary English academic, critic, and poet.

Francis Jeffrey (1773–1850) was an English critic and editor of the *Edinburgh Review,* an influential magazine dedicated to Whig political interests.

John Keats (1795–1821) was an English Romantic poet, author of "To Autumn" and "Ode to a Nightingale." He died very young, he is often regarded as the most talented poet of the Romantic generation.

Thomas de Quincey (1785–1859) was a celebrated English essayist, known for his attention to unusual topics and for the self-consciousness of his work. He is best remembered for *Confessions of an English Opium-Eater.*

Jerome McGann (born 1937) is a noted American scholar of Romanticism and nineteenth-century poetry. He is University Professor and John Stewart Bryan Professor of English at the University of Virginia.

John Milton (1608-1674) was an English writer of poetry and prose works. Milton lived through a period of enormous tumult in English politics, and many of his prose works took up political subjects; however, Milton is best known for his poetic works, including many sonnets and the epic poem *Paradise Lost*.

J. S. Mill (1806-1873) was an English philosopher and economist, known for his conception of liberty and his utilitarian ethical theory.

Alexander Pope (1688-1744) was an English poet, known for his brilliant use of classical literary imitation and his perfection of the mock-heroic style in his satirical poem "The Rape of the Lock" (1712).

John Ruskin (1819-1900) was an English writer, social thinker, philanthropist, and the leading art critic of the Victorian era.

Mary Wollstonecraft Shelley (1797-1851) was an English novelist and essayist. She is best known for her novel *Frankenstein*.

J.H. Prynne (born 1936) is an English poet, known for the experimental and often abstruse style of his poems.

William Shakespeare (1564-1616) was an English poet and playwright. Shakespeare was extraordinarily prolific, but he is best known for his sonnets and plays. Many of his best-known plays, such as *Romeo and Juliet, Macbeth, Twelfth Night*, and *A Midsummer Night's Dream* remain in continual performance, and have been translated into many languages.

Robert Southey (1774-1843) was an English poet and long-time associate of Wordsworth and Coleridge, who shared his youthful taste for radical politics. He was best known for long epic poems, though he was later judged a better prose writer than poet; and he was Poet Laureate of Britain from 1813 until his death.

Charlotte Smith (1749–1806) was a British poet, novelist, and author of children's books. As an undergraduate, Wordsworth read Smith's sonnets with admiration, and he returned to them again in 1802.

Lionel Trilling (1905–75) was a highly influential American literary critic and essayist, known for his psychological and philosophical methods.

Queen Victoria (1819–1901) was, until recently surpassed by Queen Elizabeth II, the longest-reigning monarch of the United Kingdom. Her reign was marked by economic and artistic flourishing.

Annette Vallon was William Wordsworth's lover while he lived in France, and became the mother of his child, Anne-Caroline.

Virgil (Publius Vergilius Maro, **70 BCE – 19 BCE)** was a classical Roman poet. The son of an Italian farmer, he was eventually regarded as one of Rome's greatest poets. He is best known for the epic poem *Aeneid*.

Dorothy Wordsworth (1771–1855) was a noted English diarist, best known for her Grasmere and Alfoxden journals. She lived with her brother, William Wordsworth, during the time that *Lyrical Ballads* and the Preface were conceived and published, and recent scholarship has drawn attention to her contributions to her brother's work.

WORKS CITED

WORKS CITED

Arnold, Matthew. *Lyrical Ballads: A Casebook*. Edited by Alun Richard Jones and William Tydeman. London: Macmillan, 1972.

"The Study of Poetry" and "Wordsworth," in *Essays on Criticism*. Edited by G. K. Chesterton. J.M. Dent & Sons, 1964.

Bate, Jonathan. *Romantic Ecology: Wordsworth and the Environmental Tradition*. London: Routledge, 1991.

Bialostosky, D.H. "Coleridge's Interpretation of Wordsworth's Preface to *Lyrical Ballads.*" PMLA 93 (1978), 912-924.

Broadhead, Alex. "Framing Dialect in the 1800 *Lyrical Ballads*: Wordsworth, regionalism and footnotes." *Language and Literature* 19.3 (2010), 249-263.

Bromwich, David. *Disowned by Memory.* Chicago: University of Chicago Press, 1998.

Byron, Lord. *Don Juan*. Edited by T.G. Steffan, E. Steffan and W.W. Pratt. London: Penguin, 2004.

Bloom, Harold and Lionel Trilling. *Romantic Prose and Poetry*. Oxford: Oxford University Press, 1973.

Coleridge, Samuel Taylor. *Biographia Literaria*, in *The Major Works*. Edited by H.J. Jackson. Oxford: Oxford University Press, 2000.

Collected Letters, 1785-1800, Volume I. Edited by Earl Leslie Griggs. Oxford: Oxford University Press, 2002.

Collected Letters, 1801-1806, Volume II. Edited by Earl Leslie Griggs. Oxford: Oxford University Press, 2002.

Eliot, George. *Selected Essays, Poems and Other Writings*. Edited by A.S. Byatt and Nicholas Warren. Harmondsworth: Penguin, 1991.

Eliot, T.S. "Tradition and the Individual Talent." In *Selected Prose of T.S. Eliot*. London: Faber and Faber, 1951.

Field, Barron. *Memoirs of Wordsworth*. Edited by Geoffrey Little. Sydney: Sydney University Press for the Australian Academy of the Humanities, 1975.

Hall, Cristy Lynn. "Encounters with Solitaries in Wordsworth's *Lyrical Ballads.*" South Atlantic Review 81.4 (2016), 28-44.

Heaney, Seamus. "The Triumph of Spirit." *The Guardian*, February 11, 2006.

Jarvis, Simon. *Wordsworth's Philosophic Song*. Cambridge: Cambridge University Press, 2007.

Jeffrey, Francis. "Review of Wordsworth, *Poems, in Two Volumes*." *Edinburgh Review* 11 (October 1807).

"Review of Wordsworth, *The Excursion*." *Edinburgh Review* 24 (November 1814).

Johnston, Kenneth R. "Wordsworth's Self-Creation and the *1800 Lyrical Ballads.*" In *1800: The New Lyrical Ballads*. Edited by Nicola Trott and Seamus Perry. Houndmills: Palgrave, 2001, 95-122.

Jordan, John E. *Why the Lyrical Ballads?: The Background, Writing, and Character of Wordsworth's 1798 Lyrical Ballads*. Berkeley: University of California Press, 1976.

Keats, John to George and Tom Keats, December 21, 27, 1817. *Selected Letters*. Edited by Robert Gittings. Oxford: Oxford University Press, 2002.

Lowe, Derek. " 'Poems So Materially Different': Eighteenth-Century Literary Property and Wordsworth's Mechanisms of Proprietary Authorship in the 1800 Lyrical Ballads." *Studies in Romanticism* 55 (2016), 3-28.

Mayo, Robert. "The Contemporaneity of the *Lyrical Ballads*." *PMLA*, Vol. 69, No. 3 (June 1954).

McEathron, Scott. "Wordsworth, Lyrical Ballads, and the Problem of Peasant Poetry." *Nineteenth-Century Literature* 54.1 (1999), 1-26.

McGann, Jerome. *The Romantic Ideology: A Critical Investigation*. Chicago: University of Chicago Press, 1985.

Mill, J. S. *Autobiography*. London: Penguin Classics, 1989.

Newman, Ian. "Moderation in the *Lyrical Ballads*: Wordsworth and the Ballad Debates of the 1790s." *Studies in Romanticism* 55 (2016), 185-210.Perry, Seamus. "Wordsworth and Coleridge." In *The Cambridge Companion to Wordsworth.* Edited by Stephen Gill. Cambridge: Cambridge University Press, 2003, 161-179.

Roe, Nicholas. "Politics, history, and Wordsworth's poems." In *The Cambridge Companion to Wordsworth.* Edited by Stephen Gill. Cambridge: Cambridge University Press, 2003, 196-212.

Ruskin, John to William Knight, April 3, 1883. Quoted in Stephen Gill, *Wordsworth and the Victorians*. Oxford: Oxford University Press, 1998.

Southey, Robert. *The Romantics Reviewed: Part A, The Lake Poets*, Vol. 1. New York: Harman, 1972.

Stafford, Fiona. "Introduction." *Lyrical Ballads: 1798 and 1802.* William Wordsworth and Samuel Coleridge. Edited by Fiona Stafford. Oxford: Oxford University Press, 2013.

Trott, Nicola, and Seamus Perry. *1800: The New* Lyrical Ballads. Houndmills: Palgrave, 2001.

"Wordsworth: the shape of the poetic career." In *The Cambridge Companion to Wordsworth.* Edited by Stephen Gill. Cambridge: Cambridge University Press, 2003, 5-21.

Wollstonecraft Shelley, Mary. *The Journals of Mary Shelley: Volume 2, 1814-1844.* Edited by Paula Feldman and Diana Scott-Kilvert. Oxford: Oxford University Press, 1987.

Wordsworth, Dorothy. *The Grasmere and Alfoxden Journals.* Edited by Pamela Woof. Oxford: Oxford University Press, 2002.

Wordsworth, William. Letter to Charles James Fox, January 14, 1801. *Lyrical Ballads: 1798 and 1802.* Edited by Fiona Stafford. Oxford: Oxford University Press, 2013.

Letter to John Wilson, May 24, 1802. *Lyrical Ballads: 1798 and 1802.* Edited by Fiona Stafford. Oxford: Oxford University Press, 2013.

Wordsworth's Guide to the Lakes. Edited by Ernest de Selincourt. Oxford: Oxford University Press, 1970.

"Preface" to *Lyrical Ballads: 1798 and 1802.* Edited by Fiona Stafford. Oxford: Oxford University Press, 2013

"Preface" to *Poems,* 1815. *William Wordsworth: The Major Works.* Edited by Stephen Gill. Oxford: Oxford University Press, 2000.

Wu, Duncan. "Wordsworth's poetry to 1798." In *The Cambridge Companion to Wordsworth.* Edited by Stephen Gill. Cambridge: Cambridge University Press, 2003, 22-37.

THE MACAT LIBRARY
BY DISCIPLINE

AFRICANA STUDIES

Chinua Achebe's *An Image of Africa: Racism in Conrad's Heart of Darkness*
W. E. B. Du Bois's *The Souls of Black Folk*
Zora Neale Huston's *Characteristics of Negro Expression*
Martin Luther King Jr's *Why We Can't Wait*
Toni Morrison's *Playing in the Dark: Whiteness in the American Literary Imagination*

ANTHROPOLOGY

Arjun Appadurai's *Modernity at Large: Cultural Dimensions of Globalisation*
Philippe Ariès's *Centuries of Childhood*
Franz Boas's *Race, Language and Culture*
Kim Chan & Renée Mauborgne's *Blue Ocean Strategy*
Jared Diamond's *Guns, Germs & Steel: the Fate of Human Societies*
Jared Diamond's *Collapse: How Societies Choose to Fail or Survive*
E. E. Evans-Pritchard's *Witchcraft, Oracles and Magic Among the Azande*
James Ferguson's *The Anti-Politics Machine*
Clifford Geertz's *The Interpretation of Cultures*
David Graeber's *Debt: the First 5000 Years*
Karen Ho's *Liquidated: An Ethnography of Wall Street*
Geert Hofstede's *Culture's Consequences: Comparing Values, Behaviors, Institutes and Organizations across Nations*
Claude Lévi-Strauss's *Structural Anthropology*
Jay Macleod's *Ain't No Makin' It: Aspirations and Attainment in a Low-Income Neighborhood*
Saba Mahmood's *The Politics of Piety: The Islamic Revival and the Feminist Subject*
Marcel Mauss's *The Gift*

BUSINESS

Jean Lave & Etienne Wenger's *Situated Learning*
Theodore Levitt's *Marketing Myopia*
Burton G. Malkiel's *A Random Walk Down Wall Street*
Douglas McGregor's *The Human Side of Enterprise*
Michael Porter's *Competitive Strategy: Creating and Sustaining Superior Performance*
John Kotter's *Leading Change*
C. K. Prahalad & Gary Hamel's *The Core Competence of the Corporation*

CRIMINOLOGY

Michelle Alexander's *The New Jim Crow: Mass Incarceration in the Age of Colorblindness*
Michael R. Gottfredson & Travis Hirschi's *A General Theory of Crime*
Richard Herrnstein & Charles A. Murray's *The Bell Curve: Intelligence and Class Structure in American Life*
Elizabeth Loftus's *Eyewitness Testimony*
Jay Macleod's *Ain't No Makin' It: Aspirations and Attainment in a Low-Income Neighborhood*
Philip Zimbardo's *The Lucifer Effect*

ECONOMICS

Janet Abu-Lughod's *Before European Hegemony*
Ha-Joon Chang's *Kicking Away the Ladder*
David Brion Davis's *The Problem of Slavery in the Age of Revolution*
Milton Friedman's *The Role of Monetary Policy*
Milton Friedman's *Capitalism and Freedom*
David Graeber's *Debt: the First 5000 Years*
Friedrich Hayek's *The Road to Serfdom*
Karen Ho's *Liquidated: An Ethnography of Wall Street*

John Maynard Keynes's *The General Theory of Employment, Interest and Money*
Charles P. Kindleberger's *Manias, Panics and Crashes*
Robert Lucas's *Why Doesn't Capital Flow from Rich to Poor Countries?*
Burton G. Malkiel's *A Random Walk Down Wall Street*
Thomas Robert Malthus's *An Essay on the Principle of Population*
Karl Marx's *Capital*
Thomas Piketty's *Capital in the Twenty-First Century*
Amartya Sen's *Development as Freedom*
Adam Smith's *The Wealth of Nations*
Nassim Nicholas Taleb's *The Black Swan: The Impact of the Highly Improbable*
Amos Tversky's & Daniel Kahneman's *Judgment under Uncertainty: Heuristics and Biases*
Mahbub Ul Haq's *Reflections on Human Development*
Max Weber's *The Protestant Ethic and the Spirit of Capitalism*

FEMINISM AND GENDER STUDIES

Judith Butler's *Gender Trouble*
Simone De Beauvoir's *The Second Sex*
Michel Foucault's *History of Sexuality*
Betty Friedan's *The Feminine Mystique*
Saba Mahmood's *The Politics of Piety: The Islamic Revival and the Feminist Subject*
Joan Wallach Scott's *Gender and the Politics of History*
Mary Wollstonecraft's *A Vindication of the Rights of Woman*
Virginia Woolf's *A Room of One's Own*

GEOGRAPHY

The Brundtland Report's *Our Common Future*
Rachel Carson's *Silent Spring*
Charles Darwin's *On the Origin of Species*
James Ferguson's *The Anti-Politics Machine*
Jane Jacobs's *The Death and Life of Great American Cities*
James Lovelock's *Gaia: A New Look at Life on Earth*
Amartya Sen's *Development as Freedom*
Mathis Wackernagel & William Rees's *Our Ecological Footprint*

HISTORY

Janet Abu-Lughod's *Before European Hegemony*
Benedict Anderson's *Imagined Communities*
Bernard Bailyn's *The Ideological Origins of the American Revolution*
Hanna Batatu's *The Old Social Classes And The Revolutionary Movements Of Iraq*
Christopher Browning's *Ordinary Men: Reserve Police Batallion 101 and the Final Solution in Poland*
Edmund Burke's *Reflections on the Revolution in France*
William Cronon's *Nature's Metropolis: Chicago And The Great West*
Alfred W. Crosby's *The Columbian Exchange*
Hamid Dabashi's *Iran: A People Interrupted*
David Brion Davis's *The Problem of Slavery in the Age of Revolution*
Nathalie Zemon Davis's *The Return of Martin Guerre*
Jared Diamond's *Guns, Germs & Steel: the Fate of Human Societies*
Frank Dikotter's *Mao's Great Famine*
John W Dower's *War Without Mercy: Race And Power In The Pacific War*
W. E. B. Du Bois's *The Souls of Black Folk*
Richard J. Evans's *In Defence of History*
Lucien Febvre's *The Problem of Unbelief in the 16th Century*
Sheila Fitzpatrick's *Everyday Stalinism*

Eric Foner's *Reconstruction: America's Unfinished Revolution, 1863-1877*
Michel Foucault's *Discipline and Punish*
Michel Foucault's *History of Sexuality*
Francis Fukuyama's *The End of History and the Last Man*
John Lewis Gaddis's *We Now Know: Rethinking Cold War History*
Ernest Gellner's *Nations and Nationalism*
Eugene Genovese's *Roll, Jordan, Roll: The World the Slaves Made*
Carlo Ginzburg's *The Night Battles*
Daniel Goldhagen's *Hitler's Willing Executioners*
Jack Goldstone's *Revolution and Rebellion in the Early Modern World*
Antonio Gramsci's *The Prison Notebooks*
Alexander Hamilton, John Jay & James Madison's *The Federalist Papers*
Christopher Hill's *The World Turned Upside Down*
Carole Hillenbrand's *The Crusades: Islamic Perspectives*
Thomas Hobbes's *Leviathan*
Eric Hobsbawm's *The Age Of Revolution*
John A. Hobson's *Imperialism: A Study*
Albert Hourani's *History of the Arab Peoples*
Samuel P. Huntington's *The Clash of Civilizations and the Remaking of World Order*
C. L. R. James's *The Black Jacobins*
Tony Judt's *Postwar: A History of Europe Since 1945*
Ernst Kantorowicz's *The King's Two Bodies: A Study in Medieval Political Theology*
Paul Kennedy's *The Rise and Fall of the Great Powers*
Ian Kershaw's *The "Hitler Myth": Image and Reality in the Third Reich*
John Maynard Keynes's *The General Theory of Employment, Interest and Money*
Charles P. Kindleberger's *Manias, Panics and Crashes*
Martin Luther King Jr's *Why We Can't Wait*
Henry Kissinger's *World Order: Reflections on the Character of Nations and the Course of History*
Thomas Kuhn's *The Structure of Scientific Revolutions*
Georges Lefebvre's *The Coming of the French Revolution*
John Locke's *Two Treatises of Government*
Niccolò Machiavelli's *The Prince*
Thomas Robert Malthus's *An Essay on the Principle of Population*
Mahmood Mamdani's *Citizen and Subject: Contemporary Africa And The Legacy Of Late Colonialism*
Karl Marx's *Capital*
Stanley Milgram's *Obedience to Authority*
John Stuart Mill's *On Liberty*
Thomas Paine's *Common Sense*
Thomas Paine's *Rights of Man*
Geoffrey Parker's *Global Crisis: War, Climate Change and Catastrophe in the Seventeenth Century*
Jonathan Riley-Smith's *The First Crusade and the Idea of Crusading*
Jean-Jacques Rousseau's *The Social Contract*
Joan Wallach Scott's *Gender and the Politics of History*
Theda Skocpol's *States and Social Revolutions*
Adam Smith's *The Wealth of Nations*
Timothy Snyder's *Bloodlands: Europe Between Hitler and Stalin*
Sun Tzu's *The Art of War*
Keith Thomas's *Religion and the Decline of Magic*
Thucydides's *The History of the Peloponnesian War*
Frederick Jackson Turner's *The Significance of the Frontier in American History*
Odd Arne Westad's *The Global Cold War: Third World Interventions And The Making Of Our Times*

LITERATURE

Chinua Achebe's *An Image of Africa: Racism in Conrad's Heart of Darkness*
Roland Barthes's *Mythologies*
Homi K. Bhabha's *The Location of Culture*
Judith Butler's *Gender Trouble*
Simone De Beauvoir's *The Second Sex*
Ferdinand De Saussure's *Course in General Linguistics*
T. S. Eliot's *The Sacred Wood: Essays on Poetry and Criticism*
Zora Neale Huston's *Characteristics of Negro Expression*
Toni Morrison's *Playing in the Dark: Whiteness in the American Literary Imagination*
Edward Said's *Orientalism*
Gayatri Chakravorty Spivak's *Can the Subaltern Speak?*
Mary Wollstonecraft's *A Vindication of the Rights of Women*
Virginia Woolf's *A Room of One's Own*

PHILOSOPHY

Elizabeth Anscombe's *Modern Moral Philosophy*
Hannah Arendt's *The Human Condition*
Aristotle's *Metaphysics*
Aristotle's *Nicomachean Ethics*
Edmund Gettier's *Is Justified True Belief Knowledge?*
Georg Wilhelm Friedrich Hegel's *Phenomenology of Spirit*
David Hume's *Dialogues Concerning Natural Religion*
David Hume's *The Enquiry for Human Understanding*
Immanuel Kant's *Religion within the Boundaries of Mere Reason*
Immanuel Kant's *Critique of Pure Reason*
Søren Kierkegaard's *The Sickness Unto Death*
Søren Kierkegaard's *Fear and Trembling*
C. S. Lewis's *The Abolition of Man*
Alasdair MacIntyre's *After Virtue*
Marcus Aurelius's *Meditations*
Friedrich Nietzsche's *On the Genealogy of Morality*
Friedrich Nietzsche's *Beyond Good and Evil*
Plato's *Republic*
Plato's *Symposium*
Jean-Jacques Rousseau's *The Social Contract*
Gilbert Ryle's *The Concept of Mind*
Baruch Spinoza's *Ethics*
Sun Tzu's *The Art of War*
Ludwig Wittgenstein's *Philosophical Investigations*

POLITICS

Benedict Anderson's *Imagined Communities*
Aristotle's *Politics*
Bernard Bailyn's *The Ideological Origins of the American Revolution*
Edmund Burke's *Reflections on the Revolution in France*
John C. Calhoun's *A Disquisition on Government*
Ha-Joon Chang's *Kicking Away the Ladder*
Hamid Dabashi's *Iran: A People Interrupted*
Hamid Dabashi's *Theology of Discontent: The Ideological Foundation of the Islamic Revolution in Iran*
Robert Dahl's *Democracy and its Critics*
Robert Dahl's *Who Governs?*
David Brion Davis's *The Problem of Slavery in the Age of Revolution*

Alexis De Tocqueville's *Democracy in America*
James Ferguson's *The Anti-Politics Machine*
Frank Dikotter's *Mao's Great Famine*
Sheila Fitzpatrick's *Everyday Stalinism*
Eric Foner's *Reconstruction: America's Unfinished Revolution, 1863-1877*
Milton Friedman's *Capitalism and Freedom*
Francis Fukuyama's *The End of History and the Last Man*
John Lewis Gaddis's *We Now Know: Rethinking Cold War History*
Ernest Gellner's *Nations and Nationalism*
David Graeber's *Debt: the First 5000 Years*
Antonio Gramsci's *The Prison Notebooks*
Alexander Hamilton, John Jay & James Madison's *The Federalist Papers*
Friedrich Hayek's *The Road to Serfdom*
Christopher Hill's *The World Turned Upside Down*
Thomas Hobbes's *Leviathan*
John A. Hobson's *Imperialism: A Study*
Samuel P. Huntington's *The Clash of Civilizations and the Remaking of World Order*
Tony Judt's *Postwar: A History of Europe Since 1945*
David C. Kang's *China Rising: Peace, Power and Order in East Asia*
Paul Kennedy's *The Rise and Fall of Great Powers*
Robert Keohane's *After Hegemony*
Martin Luther King Jr.'s *Why We Can't Wait*
Henry Kissinger's *World Order: Reflections on the Character of Nations and the Course of History*
John Locke's *Two Treatises of Government*
Niccolò Machiavelli's *The Prince*
Thomas Robert Malthus's *An Essay on the Principle of Population*
Mahmood Mamdani's *Citizen and Subject: Contemporary Africa And The Legacy Of Late Colonialism*
Karl Marx's *Capital*
John Stuart Mill's *On Liberty*
John Stuart Mill's *Utilitarianism*
Hans Morgenthau's *Politics Among Nations*
Thomas Paine's *Common Sense*
Thomas Paine's *Rights of Man*
Thomas Piketty's *Capital in the Twenty-First Century*
Robert D. Putman's *Bowling Alone*
John Rawls's *Theory of Justice*
Jean-Jacques Rousseau's *The Social Contract*
Theda Skocpol's *States and Social Revolutions*
Adam Smith's *The Wealth of Nations*
Sun Tzu's *The Art of War*
Henry David Thoreau's *Civil Disobedience*
Thucydides's *The History of the Peloponnesian War*
Kenneth Waltz's *Theory of International Politics*
Max Weber's *Politics as a Vocation*
Odd Arne Westad's *The Global Cold War: Third World Interventions And The Making Of Our Times*

POSTCOLONIAL STUDIES

Roland Barthes's *Mythologies*
Frantz Fanon's *Black Skin, White Masks*
Homi K. Bhabha's *The Location of Culture*
Gustavo Gutiérrez's *A Theology of Liberation*
Edward Said's *Orientalism*
Gayatri Chakravorty Spivak's *Can the Subaltern Speak?*

PSYCHOLOGY

Gordon Allport's *The Nature of Prejudice*
Alan Baddeley & Graham Hitch's *Aggression: A Social Learning Analysis*
Albert Bandura's *Aggression: A Social Learning Analysis*
Leon Festinger's *A Theory of Cognitive Dissonance*
Sigmund Freud's *The Interpretation of Dreams*
Betty Friedan's *The Feminine Mystique*
Michael R. Gottfredson & Travis Hirschi's *A General Theory of Crime*
Eric Hoffer's *The True Believer: Thoughts on the Nature of Mass Movements*
William James's *Principles of Psychology*
Elizabeth Loftus's *Eyewitness Testimony*
A. H. Maslow's *A Theory of Human Motivation*
Stanley Milgram's *Obedience to Authority*
Steven Pinker's *The Better Angels of Our Nature*
Oliver Sacks's *The Man Who Mistook His Wife For a Hat*
Richard Thaler & Cass Sunstein's *Nudge: Improving Decisions About Health, Wealth and Happiness*
Amos Tversky's *Judgment under Uncertainty: Heuristics and Biases*
Philip Zimbardo's *The Lucifer Effect*

SCIENCE

Rachel Carson's *Silent Spring*
William Cronon's *Nature's Metropolis: Chicago And The Great West*
Alfred W. Crosby's *The Columbian Exchange*
Charles Darwin's *On the Origin of Species*
Richard Dawkin's *The Selfish Gene*
Thomas Kuhn's *The Structure of Scientific Revolutions*
Geoffrey Parker's *Global Crisis: War, Climate Change and Catastrophe in the Seventeenth Century*
Mathis Wackernagel & William Rees's *Our Ecological Footprint*

SOCIOLOGY

Michelle Alexander's *The New Jim Crow: Mass Incarceration in the Age of Colorblindness*
Gordon Allport's *The Nature of Prejudice*
Albert Bandura's *Aggression: A Social Learning Analysis*
Hanna Batatu's *The Old Social Classes And The Revolutionary Movements Of Iraq*
Ha-Joon Chang's *Kicking Away the Ladder*
W. E. B. Du Bois's *The Souls of Black Folk*
Émile Durkheim's *On Suicide*
Frantz Fanon's *Black Skin, White Masks*
Frantz Fanon's *The Wretched of the Earth*
Eric Foner's *Reconstruction: America's Unfinished Revolution, 1863-1877*
Eugene Genovese's *Roll, Jordan, Roll: The World the Slaves Made*
Jack Goldstone's *Revolution and Rebellion in the Early Modern World*
Antonio Gramsci's *The Prison Notebooks*
Richard Herrnstein & Charles A Murray's *The Bell Curve: Intelligence and Class Structure in American Life*
Eric Hoffer's *The True Believer: Thoughts on the Nature of Mass Movements*
Jane Jacobs's *The Death and Life of Great American Cities*
Robert Lucas's *Why Doesn't Capital Flow from Rich to Poor Countries?*
Jay Macleod's *Ain't No Makin' It: Aspirations and Attainment in a Low Income Neighborhood*
Elaine May's *Homeward Bound: American Families in the Cold War Era*
Douglas McGregor's *The Human Side of Enterprise*
C. Wright Mills's *The Sociological Imagination*

Thomas Piketty's *Capital in the Twenty-First Century*
Robert D. Putman's *Bowling Alone*
David Riesman's *The Lonely Crowd: A Study of the Changing American Character*
Edward Said's *Orientalism*
Joan Wallach Scott's *Gender and the Politics of History*
Theda Skocpol's *States and Social Revolutions*
Max Weber's *The Protestant Ethic and the Spirit of Capitalism*

THEOLOGY

Augustine's *Confessions*
Benedict's *Rule of St Benedict*
Gustavo Gutiérrez's *A Theology of Liberation*
Carole Hillenbrand's *The Crusades: Islamic Perspectives*
David Hume's *Dialogues Concerning Natural Religion*
Immanuel Kant's *Religion within the Boundaries of Mere Reason*
Ernst Kantorowicz's *The King's Two Bodies: A Study in Medieval Political Theology*
Søren Kierkegaard's *The Sickness Unto Death*
C. S. Lewis's *The Abolition of Man*
Saba Mahmood's *The Politics of Piety: The Islamic Revival and the Feminist Subject*
Baruch Spinoza's *Ethics*
Keith Thomas's *Religion and the Decline of Magic*

Macat Disciplines

*Access the greatest ideas and thinkers
across entire disciplines, including*

Macat Pairs

Analyse historical and modern issues from opposite sides of an argument. Pairs include:

HOW TO RUN AN ECONOMY

John Maynard Keynes's
The General Theory OF Employment, Interest and Money

Classical economics suggests that market economies are self-correcting in times of recession or depression, and tend toward full employment and output. But English economist John Maynard Keynes disagrees.

In his ground-breaking 1936 study *The General Theory*, Keynes argues that traditional economics has misunderstood the causes of unemployment. Employment is not determined by the price of labor; it is directly linked to demand. Keynes believes market economies are by nature unstable, and so require government intervention. Spurred on by the social catastrophe of the Great Depression of the 1930s, he sets out to revolutionize the way the world thinks

Milton Friedman's
The Role of Monetary Policy

Friedman's 1968 paper changed the course of economic theory. In just 17 pages, he demolished existing theory and outlined an effective alternate monetary policy designed to secure 'high employment, stable prices and rapid growth.'

Friedman demonstrated that monetary policy plays a vital role in broader economic stability and argued that economists got their monetary policy wrong in the 1950s and 1960s by misunderstanding the relationship between inflation and unemployment. Previous generations of economists had believed that governments could permanently decrease unemployment by permitting inflation—and vice versa. Friedman's most original contribution was to show that this supposed trade-off is an illusion that only works in the short term.

Macat analyses are available from all good bookshops and libraries.

Access hundreds of analyses through one, multimedia tool.
Join free for one month **library.macat.com**

Macat Pairs

Analyse historical and modern issues from opposite sides of an argument. Pairs include:

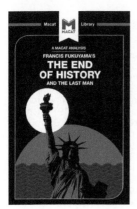

Macat Pairs

Analyse historical and modern issues from opposite sides of an argument. Pairs include: